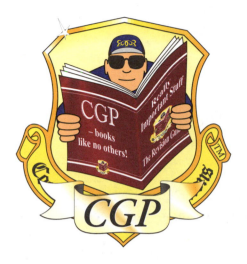

It's another Quality Book from CGP

This book is for anyone doing OCR Modular
GCSE Mathematics at Higher Level.

Whatever subject you're doing it's the same
old story — there are lots of facts and you've just got
to learn them. KS4 Maths is no different.

Happily this CGP book gives you all that important
information as clearly and concisely as possible.

It's also got some daft bits in to try and make the whole
experience at least vaguely entertaining for you.

What CGP is all about

Our sole aim here at CGP is to produce the highest
quality books — carefully written, immaculately presented
and dangerously close to being funny.

Then we work our socks off to get them out
to you — at the cheapest possible prices.

Contents

Jan '09 (Tim)

Module Nine

June '09 (Tim)

Module Ten

Jan ~~March~~ '10 (Tim)

Published by Coordination Group Publications Ltd.

Written by Richard Parsons.

Contributors: Tim Burne, Simon Little and Alison Palin.

With thanks to Charley Darbishire and Peter Caunter for the proofreading.

ISBN: 978 1 84146 550 0

Groovy website: www.cgpbooks.co.uk
Printed by Elanders Hindson Ltd, Newcastle upon Tyne

Rounding Numbers

This page shows you how to round to a certain number of <u>decimal places</u> or <u>significant figures</u>. Whichever one you're doing, the method is the same...

Rounding to *Decimal Places*

1) <u>Identify</u> the position of the LAST DIGIT.

2) Then look at the <u>next digit to the right</u> – called the DECIDER.

3) If the DECIDER is <u>5 or more</u>, then <u>ROUND-UP</u> the LAST DIGIT. If the DECIDER is <u>4 or less</u>, then leave the LAST DIGIT as it is.

<u>WORKED EXAMPLE</u>: What is 7.35 to 1 Decimal Place?

$$7.35 \qquad = \qquad 7.4$$

<u>LAST DIGIT</u> to be written (because we're rounding to 1 Decimal Place)

DECIDER

The <u>LAST DIGIT ROUNDS UP</u> to 4 because the DECIDER is <u>5 or more</u>

<u>MORE EXAMPLES</u>:

Round off 4.57 to 1 decimal place.   7 is the decider, answer is <u>4.6</u>
Round off 2.346 to 2 decimal places   6 is the decider, answer is <u>2.35</u>

Rounding to *Significant Figures*

1) The <u>number of significant figures</u> is basically just <u>how many digits</u> the number is rounded to.

2) When rounding, you usually have to <u>add zeros</u> after the <u>significant figures</u> to keep the number the <u>same magnitude</u>.

3) <u>BUT</u> don't add zeros <u>after the decimal point</u> unless they actually <u>do something</u>. E.g. 4.0317 to 3 sig fig is 4.03, not 4.0300

<u>EXAMPLES</u>:

Round off 234 to 1 sig. fig.   3 is the decider, answer is <u>200</u>
Round off 286 to 2 sig. fig.   6 is the decider, answer is <u>290</u>
Round off 2.346 to 2 sig. fig.   4 is the decider, answer is <u>2.3</u>

2 zeros needed

1 zero needed

NOT 2.300, extra zeros aren't needed.

The Acid Test

1) Round these numbers to 1 d.p.   a) 3.24   b) 1.78   c) 2.31   d) 0.46

2) Round these numbers to the stated no. of significant figures:
a) 352 to 2 s.f.   b) 465 to 1 s.f.   c) 12.38 to 3 s.f.   d) 0.03567 to 2 s.f.

Multiplying Without a Calculator

Yes it's true, you're going to have to cope without a calculator for an entire 50% of the maths exams you sit. So given that, I think you'd best get learning the next three pages...

Multiplying Whole Numbers

There are lots of methods you can use. Two of the popular ones are shown below. Just make sure you can do it using whichever method you prefer...

Example "What is 564 × 25?"

The Traditional Method:

Split it into separate multiplications, and then add up the results.

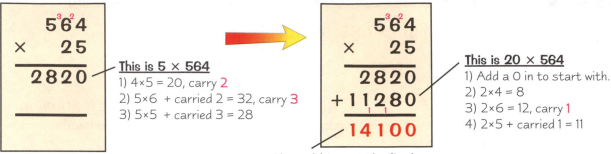

This is 5 × 564
1) 4×5 = 20, carry 2
2) 5×6 + carried 2 = 32, carry 3
3) 5×5 + carried 3 = 28

This is 20 × 564
1) Add a 0 in to start with.
2) 2×4 = 8
3) 2×6 = 12, carry 1
4) 2×5 + carried 1 = 11

Now add to get the final answer

The 'Gelosia' Method:

Arrange the calculation like below and do 6 easy multiplications to fill up the grid...

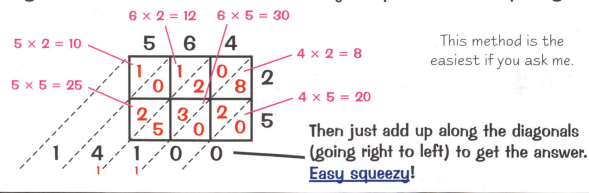

This method is the easiest if you ask me.

Then just add up along the diagonals (going right to left) to get the answer. **Easy squeezy!**

Multiplying Decimals

Learn this neat little method and you'll never be troubled by decimal points again... (probably).

1) To start with, forget about the decimal points and do the multiplication using whole numbers. (E.g. for 1.2 × 3.4 you'd do 12 × 34.)

2) Now count the total number of digits after the decimal points in the original numbers. (E.g. 1.2 and 3.4 — so that's 2 digits after the decimal point.)

3) Make the answer have the same number of decimal places.

Example: "Work out 2.68 × 3.2"

1) Ignore the d.p.s to start with: 268 × 32 = 8576

Work this out using one of the multiplication methods above.

2) 2.68 × 3.2 has 3 digits after the decimal points.

3) So the answer is **8.576**.

Dividing Without a Calculator

OK, so that's multiplication all sorted then. Now it's time for some <u>division</u>...

Dividing Whole Numbers

Again, there's lots of different methods for doing these.
Just pick one that you prefer and make sure you can do it...

Example "What is 748 ÷ 22?"

Short Division:

```
     0              0 3          Carry the 8.        0 3 4
22│ 7 4 8    →   22│ 7 4⁸8    →              22│ 7 4⁸8
```

22 into **7** doesn't go.   22 into **74** goes 3 times, remainder 8 (22 × 3 = 66).   22 into **88** goes 4 times exactly. So 748 ÷ 22 = **34**.

Long Division:

```
     0              0 3                          0 3 4
22│ 7 4 8    →   22│ 7 4 8              →     22│ 7 4 8
                   − 6 6 — 22×3                 − 6 6  Carry the 8 down.
                       8 — 74−66                  8 8
```

22 into **7** doesn't go.   22 into **74** goes 3 times.   22 into **88** goes 4 times exactly. So 748 ÷ 22 = **34**.

Repeated Subtractions:

```
22│ 7 4 8
 − 6 6 0 — Subtract 22 × 30 (22 × 3 × 10)
     8 8
 −   8 8 — Subtract 22 × 4
       0
```

So 748 ÷ 22 = 30 + 4 = **34**.

The Acid Test

It's time to test if you've <u>really learned</u> your methods for multiplication and division...

1) Have a go at these multiplications without a calculator:
   a) 28 × 12 b) 56 × 11 c) 104 × 8 d) 2.53 × 2.5 e) 3.6 × 9.6

2) Now try these divisions without a calculator:
   a) 270 ÷ 6 b) 832 ÷ 13 c) 885 ÷ 15

Dividing Without a Calculator

If you've arrived here from the previous page as is traditional, you should now be comfortable handling whole number divisions. The next thing you need to know how to do is divisions involving <u>decimals</u>. These look a bit scary, but they're fine once you know the <u>simple tricks</u>.

Dividing a Decimal by Something

Example   "What is 52.8 ÷ 3?"

Just set it out like the a <u>normal division</u> but put the <u>decimal point</u> in the answer right <u>above</u> the one in the question...

$$\begin{array}{r} 1 \\ 3\overline{)\,5\,{}^2 2\,.\,8} \end{array}$$

3 into **5** goes once, carry the remainder of 2.

$$\begin{array}{r} 1\,7\,. \\ 3\overline{)\,5\,{}^2 2\,.\,{}^1 8} \end{array}$$

3 into **22** goes 7 times, carry the remainder of 1.

$$\begin{array}{r} 1\,7\,.\,6 \\ 3\overline{)\,5\,{}^2 2\,.\,{}^1 8} \end{array}$$

3 into **18** goes 6 times exactly. So 52.8 ÷ 3 = 17.6.

If you prefer to use 'repeated subtraction' (see p3), then use the trick below for any decimal divisions...

Dividing by a Decimal

This clever method works for any division with decimals — you basically just swap it for an <u>equivalent</u> division with <u>no decimals</u> right at the <u>start</u>:

Example   "What is 83.6 ÷ 0.4?"

The trick with ones like this is to remember it's a fraction: $\dfrac{83.6}{0.4}$

Now you can get rid of the decimals by multiplying the top and bottom by 10 (turning it into an equivalent fraction): $\dfrac{83.6}{0.4} = \dfrac{836}{4}$

It's now a lovely decimal-free division that you know how to solve:

$$\begin{array}{r} 2 \\ 4\overline{)\,8\,3\,6} \end{array}$$

4 into **8** goes twice.

$$\begin{array}{r} 2\,0 \\ 4\overline{)\,8\,3\,{}^3 6} \end{array}$$

4 into **3** won't go so carry 3.

$$\begin{array}{r} 2\,0\,9 \\ 4\overline{)\,8\,3\,{}^3 6} \end{array}$$

4 into **36** goes 9 times so 83.6 ÷ 0.4 = 209.

The Acid Test

Time to test what you've learnt. Try all of these <u>without</u> a calculator:

1) 9.6 ÷ 8
2) 24.2 ÷ 2
3) 8.4 ÷ 7
4) 33.6 ÷ 0.6
5) 69 ÷ 1.5
6) 43.2 ÷ 3.6

Fractions

So you should be fairly happy doing arithmetic involving decimals now.
It's time to do the same with <u>fractions</u>.

1) <u>*Multiplying* — *easy*</u>

Multiply top and bottom separately:

$$\frac{3}{5} \times \frac{4}{7} = \frac{3 \times 4}{5 \times 7} = \frac{12}{35}$$

2) <u>*Dividing* — *quite easy*</u>

Turn the 2nd fraction <u>UPSIDE DOWN</u>
and then <u>multiply</u>:

$$\frac{3}{4} \div \frac{1}{3} = \frac{3}{4} \times \frac{3}{1} = \frac{3 \times 3}{4 \times 1} = \frac{9}{4}$$

3) <u>*Adding, subtracting* — *tricky*</u>

Add or subtract <u>TOP LINES ONLY</u>
but only if the <u>bottom numbers are the same</u>.
(If they're not, you have to make them the same – see below.)

$$\frac{2}{6} + \frac{1}{6} = \frac{3}{6}$$

$$\frac{5}{7} - \frac{3}{7} = \frac{2}{7}$$

4) <u>*Cancelling down* — *easy*</u>

<u>Divide top and bottom by the same number</u>,
till they won't go any further:

$$\frac{18}{24} \underset{\div 3}{\overset{\div 3}{=}} \frac{6}{8} \underset{\div 2}{\overset{\div 2}{=}} \frac{3}{4}$$

5) <u>*Finding a fraction of something* — *just multiply*</u>

<u>Multiply</u> the 'something'
by the <u>TOP</u> of the fraction,

then <u>divide</u> it by the <u>BOTTOM</u>:

$$\frac{9}{20} \text{ of } £360 = \{(9) \times £360\} \div (20) = \frac{£3240}{20} = £162$$

or: $\frac{9}{20}$ of $£360 = \frac{9}{1} \times £360 \times \frac{1}{20} = £162$

6) <u>**Putting Fractions *in Order*** — *put them over the same no.*</u>

E.g. Put these fractions in <u>ascending</u> order of size: $\frac{8}{3}$, $\frac{6}{4}$, $\frac{12}{5}$

① First, to find the new denominator, just
<u>multiply</u> together all the <u>denominators</u>: $3 \times 4 \times 5 = 60$

② Then change each fraction
so it's over the new number:

$$\frac{8}{3} \underset{\times 20}{\overset{\times 20}{=}} \frac{160}{60}, \quad \frac{6}{4} \underset{\times 15}{\overset{\times 15}{=}} \frac{90}{60}, \quad \frac{12}{5} \underset{\times 12}{\overset{\times 12}{=}} \frac{144}{60}$$

You can find these numbers by multiplying together the other denominators.

③ Now they're <u>easy</u> to write in order: $\frac{90}{60}$, $\frac{144}{60}$, $\frac{160}{60}$ or $\frac{6}{4}$, $\frac{12}{5}$, $\frac{8}{3}$.

The Acid Test

Do these without a calculator:

1) a) $\frac{3}{8} \times \frac{5}{12}$ b) $\frac{4}{5} \div \frac{7}{8}$ c) $\frac{3}{4} + \frac{2}{5}$

2) a) Write $\frac{27}{72}$ in its simplest form.   b) What's $\frac{7}{8}$ of £2?

3) Write these fractions in order of <u>decreasing</u> size: $\frac{1}{4}$, $\frac{2}{5}$, $\frac{3}{8}$

Calculator Buttons

In the parts of your Exam where you're allowed to use a calculator, you really need to make the most of it. It would be a disaster if you ended up throwing away easy marks simply because you pressed the wrong button.

The FRACTION BUTTON [a b/c]

You do need to know how to deal with fractions without your calculator.
But when you're allowed to use it, you definitely should do...

1) TO ENTER A NORMAL FRACTION like $\frac{1}{4}$

Just press: [1] [a b/c] [4]

2) TO ENTER A MIXED FRACTION like $1\frac{3}{5}$

Just press: [1] [a b/c] [3] [a b/c] [5]

3) TO DO A REGULAR CALCULATION such as $\frac{1}{5} \times \frac{3}{4}$

Just press: [1] [a b/c] [5] [X] [3] [a b/c] [4] [=]

4) TO REDUCE A FRACTION TO ITS LOWEST TERMS

Just enter it and then press [=] ,

e.g. $\frac{9}{12}$, [9] [a b/c] [12] [=]   [3 ⌐ 4] $= \frac{3}{4}$

5) TO CONVERT BETWEEN MIXED AND TOP HEAVY FRACTIONS

Just press [SHIFT] [a b/c]   e.g. to give $2\frac{3}{8}$ as a top heavy fraction:

Press: [2] [a b/c] [3] [a b/c] [8] [=] [SHIFT] [a b/c] which gives an answer of $\frac{19}{8}$

The MEMORY BUTTONS ([STO] Store, [RCL] Recall)

These are really useful for keeping a number you've just calculated,
so you can use it again shortly afterwards.

EXAMPLE: Find $\dfrac{840}{15+5^3}$ — just work out the bottom line first and stick it in the memory.

So press [15] [+] [5] [x³] [=] and then [STO] [M] to keep the result of the bottom line in the memory. Then you simply press [840] [÷] [RCL] [M] [=], and the answer is **6**.

(Note — memory buttons work differently on different calculators.
You must learn exactly how the memory buttons work on your calculator.)

Calculator Buttons

Bodmas and the Brackets Buttons

The BRACKETS BUTTONS are (and) .

One of the biggest problems people have with their calculators is not realising that the calculator always works things out IN A CERTAIN ORDER, which is summarised by the word BODMAS, which stands for:

Brackets, Other, Division, Multiplication, Addition, Subtraction

This is really important when you want to work out even a simple thing like $\frac{23+45}{64\times3}$

You can't just press [23] [+] [45] [÷] [64] [×] [3] [=] — it will be completely wrong.

The calculator will think you mean $23+\frac{45}{64}\times3$ because the calculator will do the division and multiplication BEFORE it does the addition.

The secret is to OVERRIDE the automatic BODMAS order of operations using the BRACKETS BUTTONS. Brackets are the ultimate priority in BODMAS, which means anything in brackets is worked out before anything else happens to it.

> So all you have to do is:
>   1) Write a couple of pairs of brackets into the expression: $\frac{(23+45)}{(64\times3)}$
>   2) Then just type it as it's written:
>
>   [( ] [23] [+] [45] [ )] [÷] [( ] [64] [×] [3] [ )] [=]

You might think it's difficult to know where to put the brackets in.
It's not that difficult, you just put them in pairs around each group of numbers.
It's OK to have brackets within other brackets too, e.g. (4 + (5÷2))
As a rule, you can't cause trouble by putting too many brackets in,

SO LONG AS THEY ALWAYS GO IN PAIRS.

The Powers Button x^y or ∧

It's used for working out powers of numbers quickly. For example to find 7^5, instead of pressing 7×7×7×7×7 you should just press [7] [x^y] [5] [=] .

The Acid Test:
Learn everything on these two pages, then practise doing it on YOUR CALCULATOR.

Use your calculator to work out the following:
1) Convert these into top-heavy fractions: a) 2 ¾ b) 16 ½ c) 8 ¼
2) Calculate the following to 2 d.p. using the brackets or memory buttons:
  a) $\frac{15+5^6}{21^3-4^3}$ b) $\frac{74^2-10^3}{\sqrt{49}\times2^4}$

Ratio

Ratio is all to do with the comparison of quantities. Compare one with another. If you increase the amount of one, you have to increase the amount of the other to keep it in proportion:

Here is the 'Golden Rule' of ratio calculation:

DIVIDE FOR ONE, THEN TIMES FOR ALL

This nifty rule helps with loads of ratio questions.

Example 1: "5 pints of Milk cost £1.30. How much will 3 pints cost?"

The GOLDEN RULE says:

DIVIDE FOR ONE, THEN TIMES FOR ALL

which means:

Divide the price by 5 to find how much **FOR ONE PINT**, then **multiply by 3** to find how much **FOR 3 PINTS.**

So.....   £1.30 ÷ 5 = 0.26 = **26p**   (for 1 pint)
            ×3 = **78p**   (for 3 pints)

Example 2: "Divide £400 in the ratio 5:3"

The GOLDEN RULE says:

DIVIDE FOR ONE, THEN TIMES FOR ALL

The trick with this type of question is to add together the numbers in the **RATIO** to find how many **PARTS** there are: 5 + 3 = **8 parts**.   Now use The Golden Rule:

Divide the £400 by 8 to find how much it is for **ONE PART**

then **multiply by 5 and by 3** to find how much **5 PARTS ARE** and how much **3 PARTS ARE.**

So...   £400 ÷ 8 = £50   (for 1 part)
        ×5 = **£250** (for 5 parts)   and ×3 = **£150**   (for 3 parts)

        So £400 split in the ratio 5:3 is   **£250 : £150**

The Acid Test

1) If seven pencils cost 98p, how much will 4 pencils cost?
2) Divide £2400 in the ratio 5:7.

Ratio

A favourite type of question they like to ask you in Exams is comparing the "value for money" of 2 or 3 similar items. Always follow the <u>GOLDEN RULE</u>...

> ## *Divide by the <u>PRICE</u> in pence*
> ## *(to get the amount <u>per penny</u>)*

Example: The local "Supplies 'n' Vittals" stocks three sizes of Jamaican Gooseberry Jam. The question is: Which of these represents "<u>THE BEST</u>

<u>VALUE FOR MONEY</u>"?

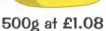

500g at £1.08   350g at 80p   100g at 42p

ANSWER: the <u>GOLDEN RULE</u> says :

> ## *DIVIDE BY THE PRICE <u>IN PENCE</u>* TO GET THE AMOUNT <u>PER PENNY</u>

So we shall:

500g ÷ 108p =	<u>4.6g PER PENNY</u>
350g ÷ 80p =	<u>4.4g PER PENNY</u>
100g ÷ 42p =	<u>2.4g PER PENNY</u>

So we can now see straight away that <u>THE 500g JAR</u> is the best value for money because you get <u>MORE JAM PER PENNY</u> (As you should expect, it being the big jar).

With any question comparing "value for money", <u>DIVIDE BY THE PRICE</u> (in pence) and it will always be the <u>BIGGEST ANSWER</u> is the <u>BEST VALUE FOR MONEY</u>.

The Acid Test

Froggatt's "Slugtail Soup" comes in three different sizes:

The <u>150g tin at 87p</u>, the <u>250g tin at £1.37</u> and the <u>Farmhouse Size, 750g at £3.95</u>.

Work out which one is the best value for money.   (And don't just guess!)

Algebra

Time for some algebra now. Don't let all these letters scare you — they're not so different from numbers really. Make sure you understand these two important methods for dealing with algebraic expressions. All they need is practice, practice, practice.

1) Multiplying out Brackets

1) The thing OUTSIDE the brackets multiplies each separate term INSIDE the brackets.

2) When letters are multiplied together, they are just written next to each other, e.g. $p \times q = pq$ (unless the letters are the same, e.g. $r \times r = r^2$).

3) A minus outside the bracket reverses all the signs when you multiply.

EXAMPLE: 1) $3(2x + 5) = 6x + 15$ 2) $p(2t - 3) = 2pt - 3p$

3) $-4(3p - 7q) = -12p + 28q$ — note both signs have been reversed — Rule 3

2) Factorising — Putting Brackets In

This is the exact reverse of multiplying-out brackets. Here's the method to follow:

1) Take out the biggest NUMBER that will go into every term.

2) Take out the highest power of any LETTER that will go into every term. E.g. if x^2 goes into each term, take out x^2 and not x.

3) Open the brackets and fill in all the bits needed to reproduce each term.

EXAMPLE 1:   Factorise $20x + 10y$

ANSWER: $10(2x + y)$

Biggest number that'll divide into both 20 and 10

There isn't a letter that goes into both terms

$2x \times 10 = 20x$ (1st term)
$y \times 10 = 10y$ (2nd term)

EXAMPLE 2:   Factorise $x^2 - 3x$

ANSWER: $x(x - 3)$

There isn't a number that goes into both terms (apart from 1)

Highest power of x that goes into both x^2 and x

$x \times x = x^2$ (1st term)
$-3 \times x = -3x$ (2nd term)

REMEMBER: 1) The bits taken out and put at the front are the common factors.
2) The bits inside the brackets are what's needed to get back to the original terms if you were to multiply the brackets out again.

The Acid Test:
LEARN the 3 Steps of how to Multiply out Brackets and how to Factorise. Cover the page and scribble them down.

1) Multiply out these brackets: a) $2(x - 2)$ b) $x(5 + x)$ c) $y(y + x)$ d) $-2(3 + z)$
2) Factorise the following: a) $5xy + 5$ b) $5a - 7ab$ c) $4x + x^2$ d) $y^3 + 2y^2$

Substituting into Formulas

BODMAS

If you're substituting into formulas, you're not going to get far without good old <u>BODMAS</u>.

<u>B</u>rackets, <u>O</u>ther, <u>D</u>ivision, <u>M</u>ultiplication, <u>A</u>ddition, <u>S</u>ubtraction

<u>BODMAS</u> tells you the <u>ORDER</u> in which these operations should be done: Work out <u>Brackets</u> first, then <u>Other</u> things like squaring, then <u>Divide</u> / <u>Multiply</u> groups of numbers before <u>Adding</u> or <u>Subtracting</u> them. This set of rules works really well for simple cases, so remember the word BODMAS.   (It's also back on page 7 if you want an example)

Example 1:   Use the formula $F = \frac{9}{5}C + 32$ to convert 15 °C from Celsius (C) into Fahrenheit (F).

Method: If you don't follow this STRICT METHOD you'll just keep getting them wrong — it's as simple as that.

1) <u>Write out the Formula</u>   e.g $F = \frac{9}{5}C + 32$

2) <u>Write it again</u>, directly underneath, $F = \frac{9}{5}15 + 32$
   but <u>substituting numbers for letters</u> on the **RHS**.
   (Right Hand Side)

3) Work it out <u>IN STAGES</u>.
   Use <u>BODMAS</u> to work things out <u>IN THE RIGHT ORDER</u>. *So do the $9 \div 5 \times 15$...*
   <u>WRITE DOWN</u> values for each bit <u>as you go along</u>. $F = 27 + 32$
                                                           ...then the $27 + 32$
                                                           $= 59$ so <u>F = 59°</u>

You also need to be able to substitute into formulas involving <u>powers</u>...

Example 2:   A mysterious quantity T, is given by: $T = (P - 7)^2 + 4R/Q$
                  Find the value of T when $P = 4$, $Q = -2$ and $R = 3$.

<u>ANSWER</u>:
1) Write down the formula: $T = (P - 7)^2 + 4R/Q$
2) Put the numbers in: $T = (4 - 7)^2 + 4 \times 3/\text{-}2$
3) Then work it out <u>in stages</u> : $= (-3)^2 + 12/\text{-}2$
                                  $= 9 + \text{-}6$
                                  $= 9 - 6 \;=\; 3$

<u>Note BODMAS in operation</u>:

<u>Brackets</u> worked out first, then <u>squared</u>. <u>Multiplications</u> and <u>divisions</u> done <u>before</u> finally <u>adding</u> and <u>subtracting</u>.

Example 3:   Calculate the value of $2x^3 + 5$ when $x = 3$.

<u>ANSWER</u>: Just substitute 3 for x: $2(3)^3 + 5$
                                   $= 2 \times 27 + 5$ powers first
                                   $= 54 + 5$ then multiplication
                                   $= 59$ and finally addition

---

 **IMPORTANT** While you're still enjoying this algebra lark, you should have a look at page 37 in Module 7. You need to know the <u>SOLVING EQUATIONS</u> stuff for <u>both Modules 6 and 7</u>, but we're saving trees by only including it in the book once.

Drawing Graphs from Equations

You'll probably have to plot a <u>straight line graph</u> in the Exam.

All straight lines have equations like this: $y = 2x + 3$, $y = 1 - x$, $y - 3x = 4$.

And this is how you plot the things...

1) Doing the Table Of Values

1) What you're likely to get in the Exam is an equation such as
"$y = x + 3$", or "$y = 3x + 2$" and a half-finished table of values:

EXAMPLE: "Complete this table of values,
using the equation $y = 2x - 7$."

x	-2	0	2	4	6
y	-11		-3		

2) Put each x-value into the equation and work out the corresponding y-value.
E.g. <u>For x = 0</u>, $y = 2x - 7 = (2 \times 0) - 7 = 0 - 7 = \underline{-7}$ etc...
... until you get this:

x	-2	0	2	4	6
y	-11	-7	-3	1	5

2) Plotting The Points and Drawing The Graph

THE METHOD:

1) <u>PLOT EACH PAIR</u> of x- and y- values from the table as a point on the graph.

2) Do it very <u>CAREFULLY</u> — and don't mix up the x- and y-values.

3) The points will always form <u>A DEAD STRAIGHT LINE</u>.
<u>NEVER</u> let one point drag your line off in some ridiculous
direction. You <u>never get SPIKES – only MISTAKES</u>.

4) If one point does look a bit wacky, <u>check 2 things</u>:
— the y-value you worked out in the table.
— that you've plotted it properly.

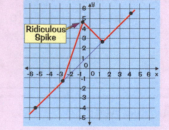

Ridiculous Spike

<u>CONTINUING THE EXAMPLE FROM PART 1)</u>:

"Use your table of values to plot
the graph of $y = 2x - 7$."

Simple — plot each point <u>CAREFULLY</u>,
then you should be able to draw a nice
<u>STRAIGHT LINE</u> through all the points.

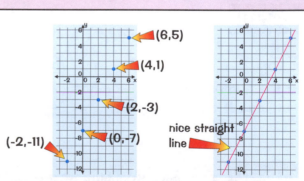

(6,5)
(4,1)
(2,-3)
(-2,-11)   (0,-7)
nice straight line

Beware — you might be given an equation with the <u>x and y terms on the same side</u>,
e.g. $y + 3x = 6$. Just <u>rearrange</u> the equation into the form $y = 6 - 3x$ before you start.

The Acid Test

x	-4	-2	-1	0	1	2	4
y	-6			-2			

1) LEARN all the important details on this page.
2) Then <u>use them</u> to <u>complete this table of values</u> for the equation: $y - x = -2$.
3) Then <u>plot the points on graph paper and draw the graph</u>.

Polygons

1) A **POLYGON** is just a fancy word for a <u>flat shape with lots of straight-edged sides</u>.
2) A **REGULAR POLYGON** is one where <u>all the sides and angles are the SAME</u>.
3) The regular polygons are a <u>never-ending</u> series of shapes — you can have one with 3 sides (an equilateral triangle), 12 sides, 25 sides or 36 sides etc.

Regular *Polygons* — *Two Formulas* to Learn...

Whenever you get a <u>Regular Polygon</u>, it's almost a <u>cosmic certainty</u> that you'll need to work out the <u>Interior and Exterior Angles</u>, because they are the **KEY** to it all.

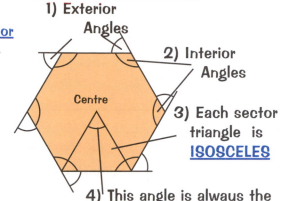

1) Exterior Angles
2) Interior Angles
3) Each sector triangle is **ISOSCELES**
4) This angle is always the same as the Exterior Angles

Centre

$$\text{EXTERIOR ANGLE} = \frac{360°}{\text{No. of Sides}}$$

$$\text{INTERIOR ANGLE} = 180° - \text{EXTERIOR ANGLE}$$

These formulas only work for <u>regular</u> polygons.

Example: Work out angles a) and b).

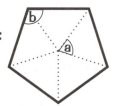

a) This angle is identical to the exterior angles, so:
   Exterior angle   = 360° / 5   = **72°**
b) This is an interior angle, so:
   Interior angle   = 180° − 72°   = **108°**

Irregular *Polygons* — *Two More Formulas*...

An irregular polygon is basically any <u>straight-sided shape</u> where the sides <u>aren't</u> all the <u>same length</u>. There are <u>two formulas</u> you need to know for them:

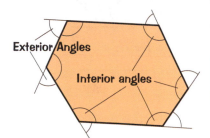

Exterior Angles

Interior angles

Sum of Exterior angles = 360°

Sum of Interior angles = (n − 2)×180°
where n is the number of sides

These formulas work for <u>any</u> polygons, regular or irregular.

The <u>(n − 2)×180°</u> formula comes from <u>splitting the inside of the polygon up into triangles</u> using full diagonals. Each triangle has 180° in it so just <u>count up the triangles</u> and times by 180°. There's always 2 less triangles than there are sides, hence the (n − 2).

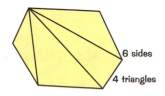

6 sides
4 triangles

The Acid Test:

1) Work out the interior and exterior angles of a regular hexagon.
2) How much do the exterior angles of a 7-sided polygon add up to?
3) How much do the interior angles of a 5-sided polygon add up to?

Parallel Lines

There's quite a few fancy names to learn on this page. But just remember, there's basically only <u>one example</u> on the page: 2 parallel lines with a line cutting them.

Whenever one line goes across <u>2 parallel lines</u>, then the <u>two bunches of angles</u> are the <u>same</u>, as shown below:

150° 30° 30° 150° 150° 30° 30° 150°

110° 70° 70° 110° 110° 70° 70° 110°

(The arrows mean those 2 lines are parallel)

> Whenever you have <u>TWO PARALLEL LINES</u>....
>
> 1) there are <u>only two different angles</u>:
>   <u>A SMALL ONE</u> and <u>A BIG ONE</u>
>
> 2) and they <u>ALWAYS ADD UP TO 180°</u>.
>   E.g.   30° and 150°   or   70° and 110°

The trickiest bit about parallel lines is <u>SPOTTING THEM IN THE FIRST PLACE</u>.

— watch out for these "Z", "C", "U" and "F" shapes popping up
  They're a dead giveaway that you've got a pair of parallel lines.

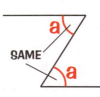

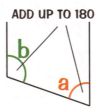

In a <u>Z-shape</u> they're called
"<u>ALTERNATE ANGLES</u>"

If they add up to 180 they're called
"<u>SUPPLEMENTARY ANGLES</u>"

In an F-shape they're called
"<u>CORRESPONDING ANGLES</u>"

Alas you're expected to learn these three silly names too!

The Acid Test

1) The diagram shown here has one angle given as 60°.
   Find all the other 7 angles.

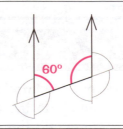

Areas

YOU MUST LEARN THESE FORMULAS:

1) RECTANGLE

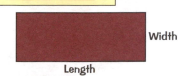

Area of **RECTANGLE** = length × width

$$A = l \times w$$

2) TRIANGLE

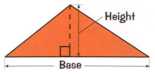

Area of **TRIANGLE** = ½ × base × vertical height

$$A = \tfrac{1}{2} \times b \times h_v$$

Note that the height must always be the <u>vertical height</u>, not the sloping height.

3) PARALLELOGRAM

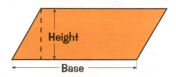

Area of **PARALLELOGRAM** = base × vertical height

$$A = b \times h_v$$

4) TRAPEZIUM

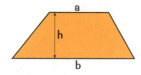

Area of **TRAPEZIUM** = average of parallel sides × distance between them

$$A = \tfrac{1}{2} \times (a + b) \times h$$

5) CIRCLE

π = 3.141592....
= **3.14** (approx)

Circumference = distance round the outside of the circle

DON'T MUDDLE UP THESE TWO CIRCLE FORMULAS!

AREA of **CIRCLE** = $\pi \times$ (radius)² e.g. if the radius is 4cm, then
$$A = \pi \times r^2$$
A = 3.14×(4×4) = **50.2cm²** (1 d.p.)

CIRCUMFERENCE = $\pi \times$ Diameter
$$C = \pi \times D$$
e.g. if the diameter is 6 cm, then
C = 3.14×6 = **18.8cm²** (1 d.p.)

YOU NEED TO KNOW THESE CIRCLE TERMS TOO:

Arcs are sections of the circle's edge...

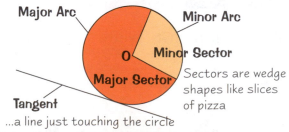

Major Arc   Minor Arc
O   **Minor Sector**
Major Sector

Sectors are wedge shapes like slices of pizza

Tangent
...a line just touching the circle

Major Segment
Chord ... a line cutting the circle
O
Minor Segment

Segments are the areas formed when the circle is chopped by a chord.

The Acid Test:

1) What are the areas of these shapes:

a)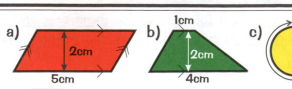
2cm
5cm

b) 1cm
2cm
4cm

c)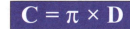

Perimeter, Area and Volume

1) Perimeters of Complicated Shapes

Perimeter is the distance <u>all the way around the outside of a 2-D shape</u>.

To find a <u>PERIMETER</u>, you <u>ADD UP THE LENGTHS OF ALL THE SIDES</u>, but....
<u>THE ONLY RELIABLE WAY</u> to make sure you get <u>all the sides</u> is this:

1) Put a <u>big blob at one corner</u> and then go around the shape.

2) <u>Write down</u> the length of <u>every side</u> as you go.

3) Even sides that seem to have <u>no length given</u> — you must <u>work them out</u>.

4) Keep going until you get back to the <u>BIG BLOB</u>.

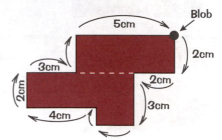

e.g. 2+2+3+2+1+4+2+3+2+5 = <u>26 cm</u>

2) Areas of Complicated Shapes

1) <u>SPLIT THEM UP</u> into their basic shapes:
   <u>RECTANGLES</u> and <u>TRIANGLES</u>

2) Work out the area of each bit <u>SEPARATELY</u>.

3) Then <u>ADD THEM ALL TOGETHER</u>
   (or sometimes <u>SUBTRACT</u> them).

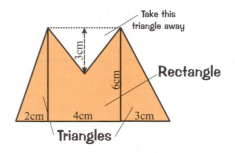

Example: Find the area of this shape.

<u>ANSWER</u>: Work out each piece of the shape separately, mark which should be added or taken away, then do the adding (or subtracting).

Triangle 1:	Triangle 2:	Triangle 3:	Rectangle:
= ½ × 2 × 6	= ½ × 3 × 6	= ½ × 4 × 3	= 4 × 6
= 6 cm²	= 9 cm²	= 6 cm²	= 24 cm²
to add	to add	to subtract	to add

So the total is: 6 + 9 − 6 + 24 = <u>33 cm²</u>.

3) Volume of a Cuboid

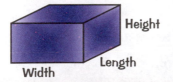

$$V = L \times W \times H$$

Volume of Cuboid = Length × Width × Height

The Acid Test:

<u>LEARN THE RULES</u> for finding the <u>perimeter</u> and <u>area</u> of <u>complicated shapes</u> and the simple <u>volume formula</u>.

1) Find the area of this shape.

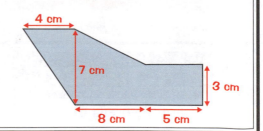

Surface Area, Nets and Projections

Surface Area and Nets

1) <u>SURFACE AREA</u> only applies to solid 3-D objects, and it's simply <u>the total area</u> of all the outer surfaces <u>added together</u>. If you were painting it, it's all the bits you'd paint!

2) A <u>NET</u> is just <u>A SOLID SHAPE FOLDED OUT FLAT</u>.

3) So fairly obviously: <u>SURFACE AREA OF SOLID = AREA OF NET</u>.

Examples:

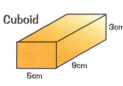

Cuboid

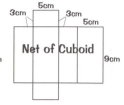

Net of Cuboid
3cm 5cm 3cm 5cm
9cm

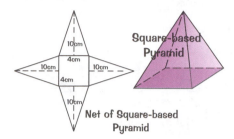

Square-based Pyramid

10cm 4cm 10cm 10cm 4cm 10cm

Net of Square-based Pyramid

SURFACE AREA OF CUBOID
= area of the 4 middle bits + the 2 flaps
= 9 × (3 + 5 + 3 + 5) + 2 × 3 × 5
= 144 + 30 = **174 cm²**

SURFACE AREA OF PYRAMID
= area of the 4 triangles + the square
= 4 × (½ × 4 × 10) + 16
= 80 + 16 = **96 cm²**

Projections show the Shape from Different Views

A '<u>projection</u>' shows the relative size and shape of an object from either the <u>front</u>, <u>side</u> or <u>back</u> — they're usually known as '<u>elevations</u>'. A '<u>plan</u>' shows the view from <u>above</u>. They're always <u>drawn to scale</u>.

Take this church (naff picture, I know) — you can represent it like this:

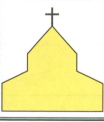

FRONT Elevation
— the view you'd see if you looked from directly <u>in front</u>:

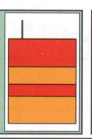

SIDE Elevation
— the view you'd see if you looked directly from <u>one side</u>:

PLAN
— the view you'd see if you looked from directly <u>above</u>:

If they're feeling really mean (and they often are), you might get a question on

This one's a bit trickier, so you might want to spend a little longer practising it — just to get your head round it.

ISOMETRIC Projection
— this is where the shape is drawn (again, to scale) from a view at <u>equal angles to</u> all three axes (<u>x, y and z</u>). Or more simply, it's a drawing like this:

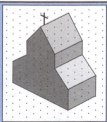

The Acid Test: Learn the simple method for finding the <u>surface area</u> of <u>solids</u> and all the details about <u>projections</u>.

1) Find the surface area of this square based pyramid.

2) Draw a plan, front and side elevations and an isometric projection of your house.

The Four Transformations

There are <u>four</u> types of <u>transformation</u> you need to know
— translation, enlargement, rotation and reflection.

Translation — ONE Detail
Enlargement — TWO Details
Rotation — THREE Details
Reflection — ONE Detail
Y (The Y doesn't stand for anything)

1) Use the word **TERRY** to remember the 4 types.

2) You must always give <u>all the details</u> for each type.

1) Translation

A translation is just a <u>SLIDE</u>. You must specify <u>how far along</u> and <u>how far up</u> the translation is.

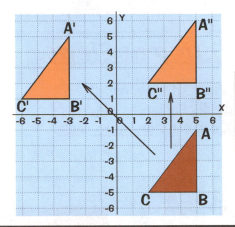

ABC to A'B'C' is a <u>translation</u> of <u>8 left and 6 up</u>.

ABC to A"B"C" is a <u>translation</u> of <u>7 up</u>.

You can describe translations with <u>vectors</u> which look like this. x is the number of spaces <u>right</u>, y is the number of spaces <u>up</u>. $\begin{pmatrix} x \to \\ y \uparrow \end{pmatrix}$

As vectors, the translations shown in the diagram are: $\begin{pmatrix} -8 \\ 6 \end{pmatrix}$ and $\begin{pmatrix} 0 \\ 7 \end{pmatrix}$

2) Enlargement

You must give these <u>2 details</u>:
1) The <u>SCALE FACTOR</u>
2) The <u>CENTRE</u> of Enlargement

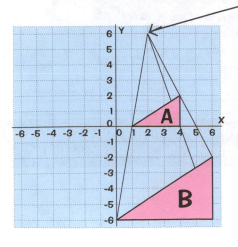

<u>A to B</u> is an enlargement of <u>scale factor 2</u>, and <u>centre (2,6)</u>

Lengths <u>doubled</u>, distance from centre <u>doubled too</u>.

If the Scale Factor is <u>smaller than 1</u> (i.e. a fraction like ½), then the shape gets <u>smaller</u>. <u>B to A</u> is an Enlargement of <u>scale factor ½</u>, <u>centre (2,6)</u>

With enlargement, the *ANGLES* of the object remain <u>unchanged</u>. The *RATIOS* of the lengths of the sides, and the object's *ORIENTATION* remain <u>unchanged</u>. The size and position <u>do</u> change.

The Four Transformations

3) Rotation

You must give these **3 details**:	1) **ANGLE** turned 2) **DIRECTION** (Clockwise or Anti-clockwise) 3) **CENTRE** of Rotation

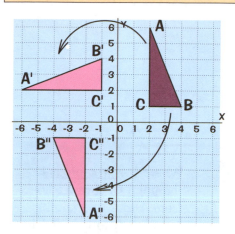

ABC to A'B'C' is a Rotation of **90°**, **anticlockwise**, **ABOUT the origin**.

ABC to A''B''C'' is a Rotation of **half a turn (180°)**, **clockwise**, **ABOUT the origin**.

(For half-turns, it doesn't actually matter if you go clockwise or anticlockwise.)

The only things that *change* in a rotation are the *POSITION* and the *ORIENTATION* of the object. *Everything else* remains *unchanged*.

4) Reflection

You must give this **ONE detail**:	1) The **MIRROR LINE**

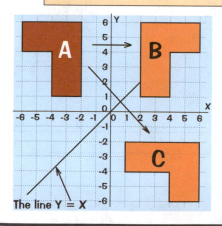

The line Y = X

A to B is a **reflection IN the Y-axis**.

A to C is a **reflection IN the line Y=X**.

With reflection, the *POSITION* and *ORIENTATION* of the object are the *only things that change*.

The Acid Test

LEARN the names of the Four Transformations and the details that go with each. When you think you know it, **turn over and write it all down**.

Describe **fully** these 4 transformations:

A → B,   B → C,   C → A,   A → D

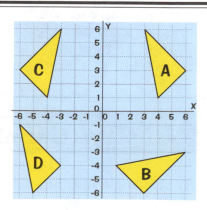

Drawing Triangles

You need to know the <u>methods</u> for accurately drawing triangles.
How you do it depends on what <u>info you're given</u> about the triangle...

Three sides — use a Ruler and Compasses

Example: Construct the triangle ABC where AB = 6cm, BC = 4cm, AC = 5cm

ANSWER: First, <u>sketch and label</u> a triangle so you know roughly what's needed. Then:

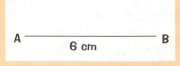

Pick a side for the <u>base line</u> — it doesn't matter which one. We'll pick <u>AB</u>. Draw a line 6cm long. <u>Label</u> the ends A and B.

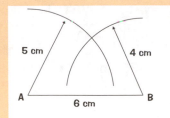

For AC, set the <u>compasses</u> to <u>5cm</u>, put the point at A and <u>draw an arc</u>. For BC, set the compasses to <u>4cm</u>, put the point at B and <u>draw an arc</u>.

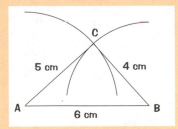

Where the <u>arcs cross</u> is the <u>point C</u>. Draw a line from A to C and another line from B to C to finish your triangle.

Sides and Angles — use a Ruler and Protractor

Example: Construct triangle DEF. DE = 5cm, DF = 3cm, and angle EDF = 40°

ANSWER: Roughly sketch and label the triangle again. Then:

Pick a side for the <u>base line</u> — again, it doesn't matter which one. I've picked DE. Draw a <u>line</u> 5cm long. <u>Label</u> the ends D and E.

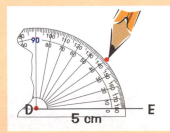

Next you have to <u>draw the angle</u> EDF (the angle at D): Place the <u>centre</u> of the protractor over D, <u>measure</u> 40° and put a <u>dot</u>.

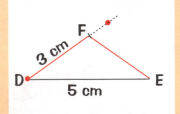

Measure 3 cm towards the dot and label it F. Now you've drawn the <u>two sides</u> and the <u>angle</u>. Just join up F and E to <u>complete</u> the triangle.

The Acid Test

1) Construct an equilateral triangle with sides 5cm.

2) Construct a triangle with sides 3cm, 4cm and 5cm. Check your drawing by measuring the sides.

3) A triangle ABC has sides AB = 8 cm, AC = 5 cm and angle BAC = 49°. How long is BC to the nearest cm? Construct the triangle to find the answer.

Probability

This is nobody's favourite subject for sure, I've never really spoken to anyone who's said they do like it (not for long anyway). Although it does seem a bit of a "Black Art" to most people, it's not as bad as you might think, but YOU MUST LEARN THE BASIC FACTS.

All Probabilities are between 0 and 1

A probability of ZERO means it will NEVER HAPPEN.
A probability of ONE means it DEFINITELY WILL.

You can't have a probability bigger than 1.

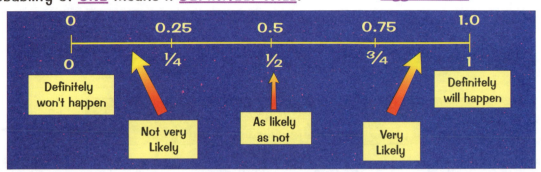

You should be able to put the probability of any event happening on this scale from 0 to 1.

Three Important Details

1) PROBABILITIES SHOULD BE GIVEN as either
   A FRACTION (¼), or A DECIMAL (0.25) or A PERCENTAGE (25%)

2) THE NOTATION "P(x) = ½" SHOULD BE READ AS:
   "The probability of event X happening is ½"

3) PROBABILITIES ALWAYS ADD UP TO 1. This is essential for
   finding the probability of the opposite happening — see below.

The Probability of the OPPOSITE happening is just the rest of the probability that's left over

Like I said — PROBABILITIES ALWAYS ADD UP TO 1. So if the probability of something happening is, say, 0.3 then the chance of it not happening is 1 – 0.3 = 0.7, i.e. what's left when you subtract the probability from 1.

Example 1: A loaded dice has a 0.25 chance of coming up TWO.
What is the chance of it not coming up TWO?

Answer: 1 – 0.25 = 0.75
So, the chance of the dice not coming up TWO is 0.75

And this method also works when there are more than two choices...

Example 2: A bag contains 4 different colours of sweets — red, green, orange and black.
A sweet is picked at random. The probability that it's red is 0.2, that it's green is
0.5 and that it's orange is 0.1. What is the probability that the sweet is black?

Answer: P(black) = 1 – P(red) – P(green) – P(orange) = 1 – 0.2 – 0.5 – 0.1 = 0.2

Probability

Calculating Probabilities

When the different results have the <u>same chance</u> of happening, then the probabilities will be <u>equal</u>. The <u>two classic cases</u> of this which tend to come up in Exams are:

1) <u>Tossing a coin</u> — Equal chance of getting heads or tails (½). —— E.g. P(heads) = ½

2) <u>Throwing a dice</u> — Equal chance of getting any of the six numbers ($^1/_6$). —— E.g. P(3) = $^1/_6$

When the results <u>aren't all equally likely</u> you have to work the probabilities out.

The <u>probability</u> of an event happening is just

$$\frac{\text{Number of ways of getting the event}}{\text{Total number of possible outcomes}}$$

EXAMPLE 1: "A bag contains 6 blue balls, 5 red balls and 9 green balls. Find the probability of picking out a green ball."

<u>ANSWER</u>: The probability of picking a green is simply:

$$\frac{\text{NUMBER OF GREENS}}{\text{TOTAL NUMBER OF BALLS}} = \frac{9}{20}$$

There are 9 ways of getting a green ball.

There are 20 possible outcomes altogether.

EXAMPLE 2:   "What is the probability of winning £45 on this spinner?"

<u>ANSWER</u>:

The pointer has <u>the same chance</u> of stopping on <u>every sector</u>...
... and since there are 2 sectors which give £45 and 8 sectors altogether, then the probability of getting £45 is $^2/_8 = ^1/_4$.

<u>REMEMBER</u> ... you can say this as a **FRACTION** or a **DECIMAL** or a **PERCENTAGE**:

1/4 is <u>0.25</u> (as a decimal) or <u>25%</u> (as a percentage)

Listing All Outcomes: 2 Coins, Dice, Spinners

A question you might get is to list all the possible results from tossing two coins or spinners, or a dice and a spinner, etc. Whatever it is, it'll be very similar to these, so <u>LEARN THEM</u>:

The <u>possible outcomes</u> from <u>TOSSING TWO COINS</u> are:

Head, Head	H, H
Head, Tail	H, T
Tail, Head	T, H
Tail, Tail	T, T

From <u>TWO SPINNERS</u> with 3 sides each:

BLUE , 1	RED , 1	GREEN , 1
BLUE , 2	RED , 2	GREEN , 2
BLUE , 3	RED , 3	GREEN , 3

So probability of e.g. BLUE, 1 is 1/9.

Try and <u>list the possible outcomes</u> **METHODICALLY** — to make sure you get them <u>ALL</u>.

The Acid Test

1)   What is the probability of picking from a shuffled deck of cards (no jokers)
       a) an Ace of any suit   b) a number less than 7   c) a red picture card?

Averages, Charts and Graphs

1) Averages — Mode, Median, Mean and Range

First things first, you need to know how to find these four key measures of average:

EXAMPLE: Find the mode, median, mean and range of this set of numbers:
2, 5, 3, 2, 6, -4, 0, 9, -3, 1, 6, 3, -2, 3

1) The MODE is simply the most common value — so it's 3.

2) The MEDIAN IS THE MIDDLE VALUE when the data is arranged in order:

-4, -3, -2, 0, 1, 2, 2, 3, 3, 3, 5, 6, 6, 9

← seven numbers this side ↑ seven numbers this side →

When there are two middle numbers like this, the median is halfway between the two middle numbers.

The MEDIAN falls between the 7 and 8th numbers which are 2 and 3, so it's 2.5.

3) MEAN = total ÷ number of items, so it's 31 ÷ 14 = 2.21

4) RANGE is the difference between max and min values, i.e. 9 – -4 = 13

p75 on "Spread of Data" shows you how to interpret these averages — have a flick forward to this page and read the top two sections. You could be asked about it in this module too.

2) Frequency Tables and Polygons

Frequency tables like this can be used to record large sets of data.

Length l (m)	Frequency
$20 \leqslant l < 30$	12
$30 \leqslant l < 40$	21
$40 \leqslant l < 50$	18
$50 \leqslant l < 60$	10

Groups here.

Number of things in each group here.

The data from frequency tables can also be displayed in graphs called frequency polygons.

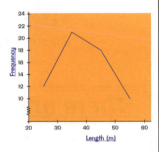

3) Stem and Leaf Diagrams

EXAMPLE: This diagram shows the ages of my school teachers.
a) How many of the teachers are in their forties?
b) How old is the oldest teacher?
c) Find the median and range of the ages.
d) Write down the modal group.

```
3 | 5
4 | 0 5 7 8
5 | 1 4 9
6 | 1 3
```
Key: 5 | 4 means 54

ANSWER:

Step 1:
Write down all the ages of the teachers, using the key.

35,
40, 45, 47, 48,
51, 54, 59,
61, 63

The key tells you how to read the diagram. A stem of 5 and a leaf of 4 means 54.

Step 2:
Answer the questions.

a) Four
b) 63

The ages are already in order, which is nice.

c) There are 10 ages, so the median is halfway between the 5th and 6th: (48 + 51) ÷ 2 = 49.5.

Range = biggest – smallest = 63 – 35 = 28.

d) Modal group is the group with the most entries. The number of groups you have depends on the number of stems. Here there are 4 stems and so 4 groups — 30-39, 40-49, 50-59 and 60-69. So the group with the most entries is 40-49.

Scatter Graphs

Scatter Graphs

1) <u>A SCATTER GRAPH</u> is just a load of points on a graph that <u>end up in a bit of a mess</u> rather than in a nice line or curve.

2) There is a posh word to say <u>how much of a mess</u> they are in — it's CORRELATION.

3) <u>Good correlation</u> (or strong correlation) means the points <u>form quite a nice line</u>, and it means <u>the two things are closely related to each other</u>. When this is the case, you can draw a <u>line of best fit</u> roughly through the middle of the scatter points.

4) <u>Poor correlation</u> (or weak correlation) means the points are <u>all over the place</u> and so there is <u>very little relation between the two things</u>. If the points are completely random, there is <u>no correlation</u> (or zero correlation).

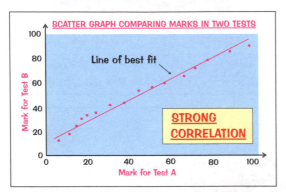

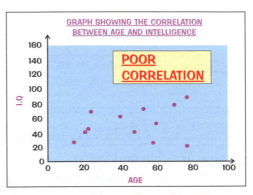

There are Names for Different Types of Correlation

1) If the points form a line sloping UPHILL from left to right, then there is POSITIVE CORRELATION, which just means that <u>both things increase or decrease together</u>.

2) If the points form a line sloping DOWNHILL from left to right, then there is NEGATIVE CORRELATION, which just means that <u>as one thing increases the other decreases</u>.

3) So when you're describing a scatter graph you have to mention both things, i.e. whether it's <u>strong/weak/zero</u> correlation and whether it's positive/negative.

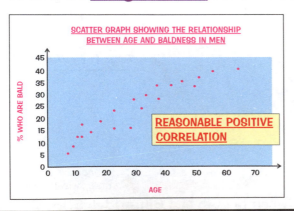

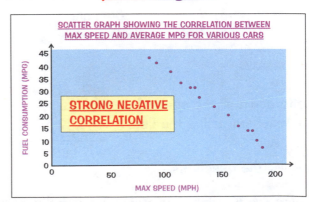

The Acid Test

1) If the points on a scatter graph are all over the place, what does it tell you about the two things that the scatter graph is comparing?

Module 7 Only

Frequency Tables

Frequency tables can either be done in <u>rows</u> or in <u>columns</u> of numbers. They can be quite confusing, <u>but not if you learn these key points</u>:

1) The word **<u>FREQUENCY</u>** just means **HOW MANY**, so a frequency table is nothing more than a <u>"How many in each group" table</u>.

2) The **<u>FIRST ROW</u>** (or column) just gives the **GROUP LABELS**.

3) The **<u>SECOND ROW</u>** (or column) gives the **ACTUAL DATA**.

4) To find the **MEAN** you have to **WORK OUT A THIRD ROW** (or column), which is equal to <u>the first row × the second row</u>.

And then **MEAN = 3rd Row total ÷ 2nd Row Total**

This will become clearer when you read through the example below.

Example

Here is a typical frequency table in **ROW FORM** and **COLUMN FORM**:

Row Form

No. of Sisters	0	1	2	3	4	5	6
Frequency	7	15	12	8	3	1	0

Column Form

No. of Sisters	Frequency
0	7
1	15
2	12
3	8
4	3
5	1
6	0

1) The <u>mode</u> and <u>range</u> are easy to find from the table:

The **MODE** is just the <u>group</u> with the <u>most entries</u>: i.e <u>1</u>
The 2nd row tells us there are people with anything from "no sisters" right up to "five sisters" (but not 6 sisters). So the **RANGE** is 5 − 0 = <u>5</u>

2) To find the <u>mean</u> for the data, you need to add a <u>third</u> row:

No. of sisters	0	1	2	3	4	5	6	totals
Frequency	7	15	12	8	3	1	0	46
No. x Frequency	0	15	24	24	12	5	0	80

<u>46</u> people were asked altogether.

There are <u>80</u> sisters altogether.

Now from the table:

MEAN number of sisters = $\frac{\text{3rd row total}}{\text{2nd row total}}$ = $\frac{80}{46}$ = <u>1.74</u> sisters per person

The Acid Test:

LEARN the <u>RULES for Frequency Tables</u>, then <u>turn over</u> and <u>WRITE THEM DOWN</u> to see what you know.

Using the methods you have just learned and this frequency table, find the **MEAN**, **MODE** and **RANGE** of the no. of phones that people have.

No. of Phones	0	1	2	3	4	5	6
Frequency	1	25	53	34	22	5	1

Revision Summary for Module Six

You've almost reached the end of the first section now, but first here's a little treat. The questions below will test how much you know and crucially what you don't know. They follow the order that the topics appear throughout the section, so it's easy to look back if you're stuck. Enjoy...

1) What are the three steps of the method for rounding numbers to a certain accuracy?

2) What three facts should you remember for rounding to a given number of significant figures?

3) Demonstrate methods for multiplying and dividing numbers without a calculator by working out:
a) 248 × 57   b) 1269 ÷ 47. Check your answers on a calculator.

4) What three rules help you multiply decimals without a calculator? Work out 23.5 × 3.76.

5) What are the rules to use for dividing decimals and dividing by decimals?
Use these to work out: a) 87.2 ÷ 4   b) 15.2 ÷ 1.6.

6) Describe in words the six rules for doing fractions without a calculator.

7) Describe the steps you'd use to order these fractions: 3/5, 6/15, 9/20, 7/10

8) Which buttons would you press on your calculator to do the following:
a) enter a normal fraction b) enter a mixed fraction c) do a fraction calculation,
d) cancel down a fraction, e) convert between mixed and top-heavy fractions?

9) When and how would you use your calculator's memory, brackets and powers buttons?

10) What is the Golden Rule for ratio questions? What's the Golden Rule for finding the "best buy"?

11) State the three rules for multiplying out brackets like 4(2t − 3p).

12) State the method for factorising (putting brackets in) expressions like $8x^2 + tx^2$.

13) Write down what BODMAS stands for and explain what it means.

14) Describe the four point method for plotting the points of a graph from an equation.

15) Sketch a regular polygon and mark on an interior and exterior angle.
Write down the formulas to calculate exterior and interior angles of a regular polygon.

16) Write down the formulas to calculate the sum of the exterior and interior angles (have a bonus point if you can explain where the interior angles formula comes from).

17) Name the two parallel lines rules and draw an example of each. Draw diagrams to show what alternate, supplementary and corresponding angles are.

18) What are the five area formulas you need to know? State the formula for the circumference of a circle. Draw labelled diagrams to illustrate these terms: tangent, arc, sector, segment, chord.

19) What are the methods for working out the perimeter and area of complicated shapes?

20) Describe how to measure the surface area of a simple 3D shape.

21) For this shape, draw the: a) front elevation b) side elevation c) plan

22) Who is TERRY and what has he got to do with transformations?
Give the details required to describe each type of transformation.

23) Describe the method for constructing a triangle when you know: a) 3 sides b) 2 sides, 1 angle.

24) Construct these triangles: a) sides 4cm, 5cm, 7cm
b) sides 7cm and 8cm and angle between them of 20°

25) Write down a) the values which all probabilities are between b) three important probability details c) how to find the probability of the opposite happening.

26) List all the possible outcomes if a dice is thrown and a coin tossed at the same time.

27) This stem and leaf diagram represents the ages of people on a bus.
Explain how you'd work out: a) the number of people on the bus
b) the mean age of everyone on the bus.

0	7,
1	5,6
2	2,4,5,8
3	0,1,1,5,7
4	0,2,5
5	6,7
6	6,
7	2,

KEY: 3|1 = 31

28) Explain what strong/weak/zero correlation are and what a positive/negative correlation means.

29) Write down the four key points about frequency tables (Hints: What does frequency mean? What do the first and second row give? How do you find the mean?)

Powers

Powers are a very useful shorthand:

$$2\times2\times2\times2\times2\times2\times2 = 2^7 \text{ ("two to the power 7")}$$
$$7\times7 = 7^2 \text{ ("7 squared")}$$
$$6\times6\times6\times6\times6 = 6^5 \text{ (" Six to the power 5")}$$
$$4\times4\times4 = 4^3 \text{ ("four cubed")}$$

That bit is easy to remember. Unfortunately, there are **SIX SPECIAL RULES** for powers that are not quite so easy, but <u>you do need to know them for the Exam</u>:

The Six Rules

The <u>first two</u> only work for powers of the **SAME NUMBER**.

1) When MULTIPLYING, you ADD the powers.

e.g. $3^4 \times 3^6 = 3^{4+6} = 3^{10}$ $8^3 \times 8^5 = 8^{3+5} = 8^8$

2) When DIVIDING, you SUBTRACT the powers.

e.g. $5^4 \div 5^2 = 5^{4-2} = 5^2$ $12^8/12^3 = 12^{8-3} = 12^5$

3) When RAISING one power to another, you MULTIPLY the powers.

e.g. $(3^2)^4 = 3^{2\times4} = 3^8$, $(5^4)^6 = 5^{24}$

4) $X^1 = X$, ANYTHING TO THE POWER 1 is just ITSELF

e.g. $3^1 = 3$, $6 \times 6^3 = 6^4$, $4^3 \div 4^2 = 4^{3-2} = 4^1 = 4$

5) $X^0 = 1$,   ANYTHING TO THE POWER 0 is just 1

e.g. $5^0 = 1$ $67^0 = 1$ $3^4/3^4 = 3^{4-4} = 3^0 = 1$

6) $1^x = 1$,   1 TO ANY POWER is still just 1

e.g. $1^{23} = 1$ $1^{89} = 1$ $1^2 = 1$ $1^{1012} = 1$

The Acid Test:

LEARN the <u>Six Rules</u> for Powers. Then <u>turn over</u> and <u>write it all down</u>. Keep trying until you can do it!

Then cover the page and apply the rules to <u>SIMPLIFY</u> these:

1) a) $3^2 \times 3^6$ b) $4^3 \div 4^2$ c) $(8^3)^4$ d) $(3^2 \times 3^3 \times 1^6) / 3^5$ e) $7^3 \times 7 \times 7^2$

2) a) $5^2 \times 5^7 \times 5^3$ b) $1^3 \times 5^0 \times 6^2$ c) $(2^5 \times 2 \times 2^6) \div (2^3 \times 2^4)$

Square Roots and Cube Roots

Square Roots

"Squared" means "times by itself" : $P^2 = P \times P$
— SQUARE ROOT is the reverse process.

The best way to think of it is this:

> "Square Root" means
> "What Number Times by Itself gives..."

Example: "Find the square root of 49"   (i.e. " Find $\sqrt{49}$ ")

To do this you should say "what number times by itself gives... 49?"
And the answer of course is 7.

Square Roots can be Positive or Negative

When you take the square root of a number, the answer can actually be positive or negative... you always have a positive and negative version of the same number.

E.g.
> $x^2 = 4$ gives $x = \pm\sqrt{4} = +2$ or -2

To understand why, look at what happens when you work backwards
by squaring the answers: $2^2 = 2 \times 2 = 4$ but also $(-2)^2 = (-2) \times (-2) = 4$

> On your calculator, it's easy to find the positive square root
> using the SQUARE ROOT BUTTON: Press $\boxed{\sqrt{}}$ $\boxed{49}$ $\boxed{=}$ = 7

Cube Roots

"Cubed" means "times by itself twice" : $T^3 = T \times T \times T$
— CUBE ROOT is the reverse process.

Note, it's twice because there are two multiplication signs.

> "Cube Root" means "What Number
> Times by Itself Twice gives..."

Example: "Find the cube root of 64"   (i.e "Find $\sqrt[3]{64}$ ")

You should say "What number times by itself twice gives... 64?"
And after a few guesses, the answer is 4.
(Note — unlike square roots, there's only ever one answer.)

> Or on your calculator just use the cube root button:
> Press $\boxed{\sqrt[3]{}}$ $\boxed{64}$ $\boxed{=}$ = 4

The Acid Test:

LEARN the 2 statements in the blue boxes and the methods for finding roots. Then turn the page and write it all down.

1) Use your calculator to find to 2 d.p. a) $\sqrt{200}$ b) $\sqrt[3]{8000}$
   For a) what is the other value that your calculator didn't give?
2) a) If $g^2 = 36$, find g.   b) If $b^3 = 64$, find b.   c) If $4 \times r^2 = 36$, find r.

Estimating and Checking

Estimating Calculations

This is quite easy. To <u>estimate</u> something this is all you do:

> **1) ROUND EVERYTHING OFF** to nice easy **CONVENIENT NUMBERS**
> **2)** Then **WORK OUT THE ANSWER** using these nice easy numbers

1) Don't worry about the answer being "wrong".
2) You're only trying to get a <u>rough idea</u> of the size of the proper answer.
In other words, is it about 20 or about 200, for example?
3) In the Exam you'll need to <u>show all the steps you've done</u>, to prove you didn't just use a calculator.

> **EXAMPLE**: *"Estimate the value of <u>127 + 49</u> and show all your working out"*
> $$\frac{127+49}{56.5}$$
>
> **Ans:** $\frac{127+49}{56.5} \approx \frac{130+50}{60} = \frac{180}{60} = 3$ ("≈" means <u>roughly equal to</u>)

Four Handy Rules...

These rules will help you spot some calculation errors <u>at a glance</u>...

> 1) *<u>MULTIPLY</u> by a number <u>LESS THAN 1</u>.* ⟶ The <u>ANSWER</u> is <u>SMALLER</u>.
> 2) *<u>MULTIPLY</u> by a number <u>GREATER THAN 1</u>.* ⟶ The <u>ANSWER</u> is <u>BIGGER</u>.

> 1) *<u>DIVIDE</u> by a number <u>LESS THAN 1</u>.* ⟶ The <u>ANSWER</u> is <u>BIGGER</u>.
> 2) *<u>DIVIDE</u> by a number <u>GREATER THAN 1</u>.* ⟶ The <u>ANSWER</u> is <u>SMALLER</u>.

EXAMPLES:

1) $32.6 \div 1.1 = 33.5$ — <u>WRONG!</u> The answer has to be smaller than 32.6.
2) $0.6 \div 0.8 = 0.75$ — Looks OK — should be bigger than 0.6 and it is.
3) $9.1 \times 1.2 = 11.83$ — Looks OK — should be bigger than 9.1 and it is.
4) $1.3 \times 1.9 = 1.8$ — <u>WRONG!</u> The answer has to be bigger than 1.9.

Be careful here — 4) tells you that the answer is bigger than 1.3 and 1.9 (because 1.3×1.9 is the same as 1.9×1.3). But 2) <u>only</u> tells you the answer is bigger than 0.6 (because 0.6 ÷ 0.8 is <u>not</u> the same as 0.8 ÷ 0.6).

The Acid Test

1) Without using your calculator, estimate the answer to this: $\frac{56.4+23.9}{36.1}$

Ratio

The whole grisly subject of RATIOS gets a whole lot easier when you do this:

Treat RATIOS *like* FRACTIONS

So for the RATIO 3:4, you'd treat it as the FRACTION 3/4, which is 0.75 as a DECIMAL.

What the *fraction* form of the ratio *actually means*

Suppose in a class there's girls and boys in the ratio 3 : 4.
This means there's 3/4 as many girls as boys.
So if there were 20 boys, there would be 3/4 × 20 = 15 girls.
You've got to be careful — it doesn't mean 3/4 of the people in the class are girls.

Reducing Ratios to their simplest form

You reduce ratios just like you'd reduce fractions to their simplest form.

For the ratio 15 : 18, both numbers have a factor of 3, so divide them by 3 —
That gives 5 : 6. We can't reduce this any further. So the simplest form of 15 : 18 is 5 : 6.

Treat them just like fractions — use your calculator if you can

Now this is really sneaky. If you stick in a fraction using the a^b_c button, your calculator automatically cancels it down when you press =.
So for the ratio 8 : 12, just press 8 a^b_c 12 = , and you'll get the reduced fraction 2/3. Now you just change it back to ratio form ie. 2 : 3. Ace.

The More Awkward Cases:

1) The a^b_c button will only accept whole numbers

So IF THE RATIO IS AWKWARD (like "2.4 : 3.6" or "1¼ : 3½") then you must:
MULTIPLY BOTH SIDES by the SAME NUMBER until they are both WHOLE NUMBERS
and then you can use the a^b_c button as before to simplify them down.
e.g. with "1¼ : 3½", × both sides by 4 gives "5 : 14" (Try a^b_c, but it won't cancel further)

2) If the ratio is MIXED UNITS

then you must CONVERT BOTH SIDES into the SMALLER UNITS using the relevant CONVERSION FACTOR, and then carry on as normal.
e.g. "24mm : 7.2cm" (× 7.2cm by 10) ⇒ 24mm : 72mm = 1 : 3 (using a^b_c)

3) To reduce a ratio to the form 1 : n or n : 1 (n can be any number)

Simply DIVIDE BOTH SIDES BY THE SMALLEST SIDE.
e.g. take "3 : 56" — dividing both sides by 3 gives: 1 : 18.7 (56÷3) (i.e. 1 : n)
This form is often the most useful, since it shows the ratio very clearly.

Ratio

Using The Formula Triangle in Ratio Questions

"Mortar is made from sand and cement in the ratio 7:2.
If 9 buckets of sand are used, how much cement is needed?"

This is a fairly common type of Exam question and it's pretty easy when you use the formula triangle method (see p48)...

This is the basic **FORMULA TRIANGLE** for **RATIOS**, but **NOTE**:

1) **THE RATIO MUST BE THE RIGHT WAY ROUND**, with the **FIRST NUMBER IN THE RATIO** relating to the item **ON TOP** in the triangle.

2) You'll always need to **CONVERT THE RATIO** into its **EQUIVALENT FRACTION** or Decimal to work out the answer.

The formula triangle for the mortar question is shown below and the trick is to replace the **RATIO** 7:2 by its **EQUIVALENT FRACTION**: 7/2, or 3.5 as a decimal (7÷2)

So, <u>covering up cement in the triangle</u>, gives us "cement = sand / (7:2)"
i.e. "9 / 3.5" = 9 ÷ 3.5 = 2.57 or about <u>2½ buckets of cement</u>.

Proportional Division

In a <u>proportional division question</u> a **TOTAL AMOUNT** is to be <u>split in a certain ratio</u>.

For example: "£9100 is to be split in the ratio 2:4:7. Find the 3 amounts".

The key word here is **PARTS** — concentrate on "parts" and it all becomes quite painless:

1) **ADD UP THE PARTS**:
The ratio 2:4:7 means there will be a total of 13 *parts*   i.e. 2+4+7 = <u>13 PARTS</u>

2) **FIND THE AMOUNT FOR ONE *"PART"***
Just divide the <u>total amount</u> by the number of <u>parts</u>:   £9100 ÷ 13 = <u>£700</u>   (= 1 PART)

3) **HENCE FIND THE THREE AMOUNTS**:
2 parts = 2×700 = <u>£1400</u>,   4 parts = 4×700 = <u>£2800</u>,   7 parts = <u>£4900</u>

The Acid Test:

LEARN the <u>6 RULES for SIMPLIFYING</u>, the **FORMULA TRIANGLE for Ratios** (plus 2 points), and the <u>3 Steps for PROPORTIONAL DIVISION</u>.

Now <u>turn over</u> and <u>write down what you've learned</u>. Try again <u>until you can do it</u>.

1) Simplify: a) 25:35   b) 3.4 : 5.1   c) 2¼ : 3¾
2) Porridge and ice-cream are mixed in the ratio 7:4 . How much porridge should go with 10 bowls of ice-cream?   3) Divide £8400 in the ratio 5:3:4

Percentage Problems

Percentage questions aren't too bad as long as you remember a couple of important points.

Two *Important* Details:

1) "Per cent" means "out of 100"

so <u>20%</u> means "20 out of 100" = <u>20 ÷ 100</u> = $\frac{20}{100}$

(That's how you work it out in the method shown above)

2) "OF" means "×"

In maths, the word "of" can always be replaced with "×" for working out the answer (as shown in the above method)

Example A radio is priced at £8.50 but there is a discount of 20% available. Find the reduced price of the radio.

ANSWER:

1) 20% of £8.50

2) $\frac{20}{100}$ × 8.5

3) [20] [÷] [100] [×] [8.5] [=] 1.7 = <u>£1.70</u>

It's money, so 1.7 on the calculator display is £1.70.

£1.70 is the <u>discount</u> so <u>subtract it</u> to get the final answer: £8.50 – £1.70 = <u>£6.80</u>

Example A plumber's bill for fixing a small leak is £98 + VAT. The VAT is charged at 17.5%. **WORK OUT THE TOTAL BILL.**

ANSWER:

1) 17.5% of £98

2) $\frac{17.5}{100}$ × 98

3) [17.5] [÷] [100] [×] [98] [=] 17.15 = <u>£17.15</u>

This £17.15 is the VAT which then has to be <u>added</u> to the £98 to give the <u>final bill</u>: £98 + £17.15 = <u>£115.15</u>

The Acid Test: LEARN the <u>two important</u> details for percentages.

1) A signed photo of Ali P the inept crocodile-wrestler is £65 + VAT at 22%. Find the total cost.

2) A signed photo of inept adventurer Tim B is £0.75 incl. VAT. It is given an 80% discount. Find the price after discount.

Prime Numbers

1) Basically, PRIME Numbers don't divide by anything

And that's the best way to think of them.   (Strictly, they divide by themselves and 1.)
So prime numbers are all the numbers that don't come up in times tables:

| 2 | 3 | 5 | 7 | 11 | 13 | 17 | 19 | 23 | 29 | 31 | 37 | ... |

As you can see, they're an awkward-looking bunch (that's because they don't divide by anything!).   For example:

The only numbers that multiply to give 7 are 1 × 7
The only numbers that multiply to give 31 are 1 × 31

In fact the only way to get ANY PRIME NUMBER is 1 × ITSELF

2) They End in 1, 3, 7 or 9

1) 1 is NOT a prime number.

2) The first four prime numbers are 2, 3, 5 and 7.

3) Prime numbers end in 1, 3, 7 or 9
(2 and 5 are the only exceptions to this rule).

4) But NOT ALL numbers ending in 1, 3, 7 or 9
are primes, as shown here:
(Only the circled ones are primes)

3) How to Find Prime Numbers — a very simple method

For a chosen number to be a prime:

> 1)   It must end in 1, 3, 7, or 9.
> 2)   It WON'T DIVIDE by any of the primes below the value of its own square root.

Example: "Decide whether or not 233 is a prime number."

1) Does it end in 1, 3, 7 or 9?   Yes

2) Find its square root: $\sqrt{233} = 15.264$

3) List all primes which are less than this square root: 2, 3, 5, 7, 11 and 13

4) Divide all of these primes into the number under test:

$233 ÷ 3 = 77.6667$ $233 ÷ 7 = 33.2857$ (it obviously won't
$233 ÷ 11 = 21.181818$ $233 ÷ 13 = 17.923077$ divide by 2 or 5.)

5) Since none of these divide cleanly into 233 then it is a prime number.   Easy peasy.

The Acid Test: LEARN the main points in ALL 3 SECTIONS above.

Now cover the page and write down everything you've just learned.

1) Find all the prime numbers between a) 100 and 110   b) 200 and 210 c) 500 and 510

HCF, LCM and Prime Fa

More fairly easy number stuff here, meaning easy marks in the E=

LCM — "Lowest Common Multiple"

The **MULTIPLES** of a number are simply its **TIMES TABLE**.
e.g. the multiples of 13 are 13   26   30   52   65   78   91

"LOWEST COMMON MULTIPLE" sounds kind of complicated but all

> The **SMALLEST** number that will **DIVIDE B**
> **ALL** the numbers in question.

Example   Find the lowest common multiple (LCM) of 6 and 7

Answer   Multiples of 6 are: 6, 12, 18, 24, 30, 36, (42,) 48

Multiples of 7 are: 7, 14, 21, 28, 35, (42,) 49, 56

So the lowest common multiple (LCM) of 6 and 7 is 42.

HCF — "Highest Common Factor"

The **FACTORS** of a number are all the numbers that **DIVIDE INTO IT**,
e.g. the factors of 12 are 1, 2, 3, 4, 6 and 12.

"HIGHEST COMMON FACTOR" — all it means is this:

> The **BIGGEST** number that will **DIVIDE INTO**
> **ALL** the numbers in question.

Example   Find the highest common factor (HCF) of 36, 54, and 72

Answer   Factors of 36 are: 1, 2, 3, 4, 6, 9, 12, (18,) 36

Factors of 54 are: 1, 2, 3, 6, 9, (18,) 27, 54

Factors of 72 are: 1, 2, 3, 4, 6, 8, 9, 12, (18,) 24,

So the highest common factor (HCF) of 36, 54 and 72 is 18.

Finding Prime Factors

Any number can be broken down into a string of prime numbers all multiplied together — this is called "Expressing it as a product of prime factors".

The mildly entertaining "Factor Tree" method is best, where you start at the top and split your number off into factors as shown. Each time you get a prime, you ring it and you finally end up with all the prime factors, which you can then arrange in order.

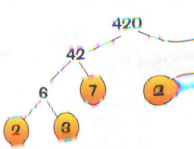

So, "As a product of pr
420 = 2×2×3×5×7

The Acid Test:

LEARN what LCM and HCF are, and the massive entertaining Factor Tree.   Turn over and write i

1) What's the LCM of 6 and 9?   2) What's the HCF of 36 and 84?
3) Express as a product of prime factors: a) 990   b) 160.

Ratio

Using The Formula Triangle in Ratio Questions

"Mortar is made from sand and cement in the ratio 7:2.
If 9 buckets of sand are used, how much cement is needed?"

This is a fairly common type of Exam question and it's pretty easy when you use the formula triangle method (see p48)...

This is the basic **FORMULA TRIANGLE** for **RATIOS**, but **NOTE**:

1) **THE RATIO MUST BE THE RIGHT WAY ROUND**, with the **FIRST NUMBER IN THE RATIO** relating to the item **ON TOP** in the triangle.

2) You'll always need to **CONVERT THE RATIO** into its **EQUIVALENT FRACTION** or Decimal to work out the answer.

The formula triangle for the mortar question is shown below and the trick is to replace the RATIO 7:2 by its EQUIVALENT FRACTION: 7/2, or 3.5 as a decimal (7÷2)

So, <u>covering up cement in the triangle</u>, gives us "cement = sand / (7:2)"
i.e. "9 / 3.5" = 9 ÷ 3.5 = 2.57 or about <u>2½ buckets of cement</u>.

Proportional Division

In a <u>proportional division question</u> a **TOTAL AMOUNT** is to be <u>split in a certain ratio</u>.

For example: "£9100 is to be split in the ratio 2:4:7. Find the 3 amounts".

The key word here is **PARTS** — concentrate on "parts" and it all becomes quite painless:

1) ADD UP THE PARTS:
The ratio 2:4:7 means there will be a total of 13 *parts* i.e. 2+4+7 = <u>13 PARTS</u>

2) FIND THE AMOUNT FOR ONE "PART"
Just divide the <u>total amount</u> by the number of <u>parts</u>: £9100 ÷ 13 = <u>£700</u> (= 1 PART)

3) HENCE FIND THE THREE AMOUNTS:
2 parts = 2×700 = <u>£1400</u>, 4 parts = 4×700 = <u>£2800</u>, 7 parts = <u>£4900</u>

The Acid Test:

LEARN the <u>6 RULES for SIMPLIFYING</u>, the <u>FORMULA TRIANGLE for Ratios</u> (plus 2 points), and the <u>3 Steps for PROPORTIONAL DIVISION</u>.

Now <u>turn over</u> and <u>write down what you've learned</u>. Try again <u>until you can do it</u>.

1) Simplify: a) 25:35   b) 3.4 : 5.1   c) 2¼ : 3¾

2) Porridge and ice-cream are mixed in the ratio 7:4 . How much porridge should go with 10 bowls of ice-cream?   3) Divide £8400 in the ratio 5:3:4

Percentage Problems

Percentage questions aren't too bad as long as you remember a couple of important points.

Two *Important* Details:

1) "Per cent" means "out of 100"

so **20%** means "20 out of 100" = $20 \div 100 = \frac{20}{100}$

(That's how you work it out in the method shown above)

2) "OF" means "×"

In maths, the word "of" can always be replaced with "×" for working out the answer (as shown in the above method)

Example A radio is priced at £8.50 but there is a discount of 20% available. Find the reduced price of the radio.

ANSWER:

1) 20% of £8.50

2) $\frac{20}{100} \times 8.5$

3) 20 ÷ 100 × 8.5 = 1.7 = **£1.70**

It's money, so 1.7 on the calculator display is £1.70.

£1.70 is the <u>discount</u> so <u>subtract it</u> to get the final answer: £8.50 − £1.70 = **£6.80**

Example A plumber's bill for fixing a small leak is £98 + VAT. The VAT is charged at 17.5%. WORK OUT THE TOTAL BILL.

ANSWER:

1) 17.5% of £98

2) $\frac{17.5}{100} \times 98$

3) 17.5 ÷ 100 × 98 = 17.15 = **£17.15**

This £17.15 is the VAT which then has to be <u>added</u> to the £98 to give the <u>final bill</u>: £98 + £17.15 = **£115.15**

The Acid Test: LEARN the <u>two important</u> details for percentages.

1) A signed photo of Ali P the inept crocodile-wrestler is £65 + VAT at 22%. Find the total cost.

2) A signed photo of inept adventurer Tim B is £0.75 incl. VAT. It is given an 80% discount. Find the price after discount.

Prime Numbers

1) Basically, PRIME Numbers don't divide by anything

And that's the best way to think of them.   (Strictly, they divide by themselves and 1.)

So prime numbers are all the numbers that don't come up in times tables:

| 2 | 3 | 5 | 7 | 11 | 13 | 17 | 19 | 23 | 29 | 31 | 37 | ... |

As you can see, they're an awkward-looking bunch (that's because they don't divide by anything!).   For example:

> The only numbers that multiply to give 7 are 1 × 7
> The only numbers that multiply to give 31 are 1 × 31

In fact the only way to get ANY PRIME NUMBER is 1 × ITSELF

2) They End in 1, 3, 7 or 9

1) 1 is NOT a prime number.

2) The first four prime numbers are 2, 3, 5 and 7.

3) Prime numbers end in 1, 3, 7 or 9
(2 and 5 are the only exceptions to this rule).

4) But NOT ALL numbers ending in 1, 3, 7 or 9
are primes, as shown here:
(Only the circled ones are primes)

```
 (2)  (3)  (5)  (7)
(11) (13) (17) (19)
 21  (23)  27  (29)
(31)  33  (37)  39
(41) (43) (47)  49
 51  (53)  57  (59)
(61)  63  (67)  69
```

3) How to Find Prime Numbers — a very simple method

For a chosen number to be a prime:

> 1)   It must end in 1, 3, 7, or 9.
> 2)   It WON'T DIVIDE by any of the primes
>   below the value of its own square root.

Example: "Decide whether or not 233 is a prime number."

1) Does it end in 1, 3, 7 or 9?   Yes

2) Find its square root: $\sqrt{233}$ = 15.264

3) List all primes which are less than this square root: 2, 3, 5, 7, 11 and 13

4) Divide all of these primes into the number under test:

233 ÷ 3 = 77.6667   233 ÷ 7 = 33.2857   (it obviously won't
233 ÷ 11 = 21.181818   233 ÷ 13 = 17.923077   divide by 2 or 5.)

5) Since none of these divide cleanly into 233 then it is a prime number.   Easy peasy.

The Acid Test: LEARN the main points in ALL 3 SECTIONS above.

Now cover the page and write down everything you've just learned.

1) Find all the prime numbers between a) 100 and 110   b) 200 and 210 c) 500 and 510

HCF, LCM and Prime Factors

More fairly easy number stuff here, meaning easy marks in the Exam if you learn it all...

LCM — "Lowest Common Multiple"

The MULTIPLES of a number are simply its TIMES TABLE,
    e.g. the multiples of 13 are 13 26 39 52 65 78 91 104 ...

"LOWEST COMMON MULTIPLE" sounds kind of complicated but all it means is this:

> The SMALLEST number that will DIVIDE BY
> ALL the numbers in question.

Example   Find the lowest common multiple (LCM) of 6 and 7
Answer   Multiples of 6 are: 6, 12, 18, 24, 30, 36, (42,) 48, 54, 60, 66, ...
           Multiples of 7 are: 7, 14, 21, 28, 35, (42,) 49, 56, 63, 70, 77, ...

So the lowest common multiple (LCM) of 6 and 7 is 42.

HCF — "Highest Common Factor"

The FACTORS of a number are all the numbers that DIVIDE INTO IT,
    e.g. the factors of 12 are 1, 2, 3, 4, 6 and 12.

"HIGHEST COMMON FACTOR" — all it means is this:

> The BIGGEST number that will DIVIDE INTO
> ALL the numbers in question.

Example   Find the highest common factor (HCF) of 36, 54, and 72
Answer   Factors of 36 are: 1, 2, 3, 4, 6, 9, 12, (18,) 36
           Factors of 54 are: 1, 2, 3, 6, 9, (18,) 27, 54
           Factors of 72 are: 1, 2, 3, 4, 6, 8, 9, 12, (18,) 24, 36, 72

So the highest common factor (HCF) of 36, 54 and 72 is 18. Easy innit...

Finding Prime Factors

Any number can be broken down into a string of prime numbers all multiplied together — this is called "Expressing it as a product of prime factors".

The mildly entertaining "Factor Tree" method is best, where you start at the top and split your number off into factors as shown.   Each time you get a prime, you ring it and you finally end up with all the prime factors, which you can then arrange in order.

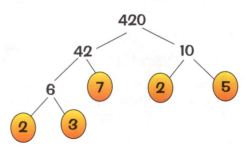

So, "As a product of prime factors",
420 = 2×2×3×5×7

The Acid Test: LEARN what LCM and HCF are, and the massively entertaining Factor Tree. Turn over and write it all down.

1) What's the LCM of 6 and 9?   2) What's the HCF of 36 and 84?
3) Express as a product of prime factors: a) 990   b) 160.

Number Sequences

"State the rule for extending the pattern"

This is what a lot of <u>Exam questions</u> end up asking for and it's easy enough, just remember:

ALWAYS say what you do to the <u>PREVIOUS TERMS</u> to get the next term.

Examples:

| 1 | 1 | 2 | 3 | 5 | 8 | 13 | ... |

1+1 1+2 2+3 3+5 5+8 8+13

The RULE:
"Add the previous two terms"

| 53 | 43 | 34 | 26 | 19 | ... |

-10   -9   -8   -7   -6

The RULE:
"Subtract from the <u>previous term</u> the difference between <u>the previous two terms</u> less one."

Finding the nth number:

This is the other common type of question. It's not hard because there's an easy formula:

$$"dn + (a - d)"$$

"d" is just **THE DIFFERENCE** between each pair of numbers.

"a" is just **THE FIRST NUMBER** in the sequence.

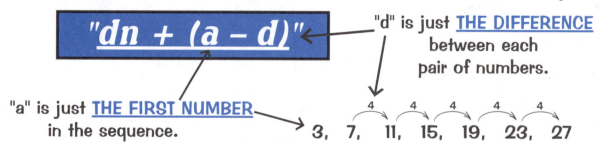

3, 7, 11, 15, 19, 23, 27 (each +4)

To get the <u>nth term</u>, you just <u>find the values of "a" and "d"</u> from the sequence and <u>stick them in the formula</u>. You don't replace n though — that wants to stay as n.

Example:
"Find the nth number of this sequence: 5, 8, 11, 14 ...."

ANS:
1) The formula is dn + (a – d)
2) The first number is 5, so <u>a = 5</u>. The differences are 3 so <u>d = 3</u>
3) Putting these in the formula gives: 3n + (5 – 3) = 3n + 2

So the <u>nth number for this sequence is given by</u>:   "<u>3n + 2</u>"

The Acid Test

LEARN the <u>5 types of number patterns</u> and the formula for finding the nth number.

1) Find the next two numbers in each of these sequences, and say <u>in words</u> what the rule is for extending each one:
   a) 2, 5, 9, 14 ....   b) 2, 20, 200 ....   c) 64, 32, 16, 8 ...

2) Find the expression for the nth number in this sequence: 7, 9, 11, 13

Making Formulas from Words

These can seem a bit confusing but they're not as bad as they look, once you know the "tricks of the trade", as it were. There are <u>two</u> main types.

Type 1

In this type there are <u>instructions about what to do with a number</u> and you have to write it as a <u>formula</u>. The only things they're likely to want you to do in the formula are:

1) Multiply x   2) Divide x   3) Square x (x^2)   4) Add or subtract a number

EXAMPLE 1:   " To find y, multiply x by three and then subtract four"

ANSWER: Start with x   →   3x   →   3x – 4   so $y = 3x - 4$

Times it by 3   Subtract 4   (not too gruelling, is it?)

EXAMPLE 2:   "To find y, square x, divide this by three and then subtract seven. Write a formula for y."

ANSWER: Start with x   → x^2 → $\dfrac{x^2}{3}$ → $\dfrac{x^2}{3} - 7$ so $y = \dfrac{x^2}{3} - 7$

Square it   Divide it by 3   Subtract 7

And now for the **SUBSTITUTION** bit... "Find the value of y when x = 3."

ANS: Write out the formula — $y = x^2/3 - 7$
Substitute in **3** for x — $y = 3^2/3 - 7$
$y = 9/3 - 7$
$y = 3 - 7$
$y = -4$

Remember, you work out the order for these things using BODMAS
Other — $3^2 = 9$
Division — 9/3 = 3
Subtraction — 3 – 7 = –4

Type 2

This is a bit harder. <u>You have to make up a formula</u> by putting in letters like "C" for "<u>cost</u>" or "n" for "<u>number of something-or-others</u>". Although it may look confusing the formulas always turn out to be <u>REALLY SIMPLE</u>, so make sure you give it a go.

EXAMPLE: To hire one of Tim's Kayaks costs £3 an hour + a fixed charge of £5. Write a formula for the total cost, T, of hiring one kayak for n hours.

Answer:
In words the formula is: Total Cost = (3 × number of hours) + 5
Putting the letters in: T = (3 × n) + 5   or better still: $T = 3n + 5$

The Acid Test

1) The value of y is found by taking x, multiplying it by five and then subtracting three. Write down a formula for y in terms of x. Work out the value of y when x = –2.

2) Hobnails produce a vast range of products including their widely-acclaimed "Hobnail Soup" which costs 95p a tin. Write a formula for the total cost C pence of buying n tins of Hobnail Soup.

Solving Equations

Solving Equations

Here's the <u>method</u> for solving equations. It's great — so make sure you <u>learn</u> it.

> 1) Always do the <u>SAME</u> thing to <u>both sides of the equation</u>.
> 2) To get rid of something, do the <u>opposite</u>.
>   The opposite of + is − and the opposite of − is +.
>   The opposite of × is ÷ and the opposite of ÷ is ×.
> 3) Keep going until you have a letter <u>on its own</u>.

EXAMPLE 1:

Solve $\dfrac{2x - 3}{5} = 3$

$$\dfrac{2x - 3}{5} = 3$$

The opposite of ÷5 is ×5 so multiply both sides by 5

$$2x - 3 = 15$$

The opposite of −3 is +3 so add 3 to both sides

$$2x = 18$$

The opposite of ×2 is ÷2 so divide both sides by 2

$$\underline{x = 9}$$

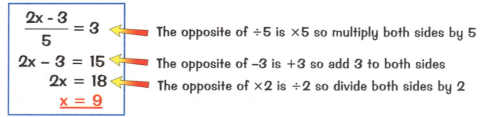

Choose the x-term and number-term to subtract which leave you with positive terms on both sides.

EXAMPLE 2 — LETTERS ON BOTH SIDES:

Solve $8x + 4 = 2x + 22$

$$8x + 4 = 2x + 22$$

Subtract 2x from both sides

$$6x + 4 = 22$$

Subtract 4 from both sides

$$6x = 18$$

Divide both sides by 6

$$\underline{x = 3}$$

EXAMPLE 3 — WITH BRACKETS:

Solve $3(2x + 1) = 4x - 1$

$$3(2x + 1) = 4x - 1$$

Multiply out the brackets

$$6x + 3 = 4x - 1$$

Subtract 4x from both sides

$$2x + 3 = -1$$

Subtract 3 from both sides

$$2x = -4$$

Divide both sides by 2

$$\underline{x = -2}$$

Rearranging Formulas

You do this in exactly the same way that you solve equations — watch...

EXAMPLE:

"Rearrange the formula $q = 3p + 4$ to make p the subject."

The opposite of +4 is −4 so take 4 from both sides

The opposite of ×3 is ÷3 so divide both sides by 3

$$q = 3p + 4$$
$$q - 4 = 3p$$
$$\underline{\dfrac{q - 4}{3} = p}$$

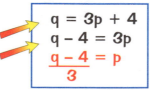

Remember, you're trying to get p on its own.

The Acid Test

1) Solve these equations: a) $2(x - 3) = -7$ b) $3(x + 1) = 2x + 8$

2) Rearrange this formula to make b the subject: $2(b - 3) = a$

Algebra

"Expanding out brackets" just means "multiplying brackets together",   e.g. $(x + 3)(x + 2)$.
This can get quite tricky and it's all too easy to get it wrong.
Learn these two very handy methods and always use one or the other:

The Jolly Old "Area" Method

The idea here is to imagine the result of multiplying two brackets as being like an area.
This is done by looking at something like $(x + 3)(x + 2)$, and thinking of it as a
rectangle which is "$(x + 3)$ long" by "$(x + 2)$ wide". Like so:

	X	**+ 3**
X	This bit is x long by x wide: AREA x^2	This bit is 3 long by x wide: AREA $3x$
+2	This bit is x long by 2 wide: AREA $2x$	This bit is 3 long by 2 wide: AREA 6

MULTIPLY to get each of the 4 BITS, ... and then ADD the 4 bits together...

... and you get the "area" of the entire $(x + 3)(x + 2)$ rectangle:
$$x^2 + 3x + 2x + 6 = x^2 + 5x + 6$$

The Fiendish Foil Method

The other method, which is a more "grown up" method, is to just multiply each of the
four bits straight off without using the area idea or drawing any boxes.

For reasons which should be quickly obvious we call this the FOIL method.

Firsts: $(x + 3) (x + 2)$ <small>times</small>

Outsides: $(x + 3) (x + 2)$ <small>times</small>

Insides: $(x + 3) (x + 2)$ <small>times</small>

Lasts: $(x + 3) (x + 2)$ <small>times</small>

So we end up with

$F + O + I + L =$

$x^2 + 2x + 3x + 6 =$

$x^2 + 5x + 6$ (again)

Try and get the hang of this FOIL method — it's much quicker than the area method once you've got it sussed.

The Acid Test: LEARN both the area and foil methods of expanding. Then turn over and scribble them down.

Then choose one of them and expand the following:
1) $(x + 1)(x + 7)$;   2) $(x - 1)(x + 3)$;   3) $(x + 6)(x - 2)$;   4) $(x - 4)(x - 5)$.

Quadratic Graphs

Equations with an <u>x² term</u> as the highest power are called <u>quadratic</u> equations. The graphs of these equations always have the same <u>SYMMETRICAL bucket shape</u>.

If the x² bit is positive (i.e. +x²) the bucket is the normal way up, but if the x² bit has a "minus" in front of it (i.e. −x²) then the bucket is <u>upside down</u>.

The graphs get steeper and steeper but <u>never vertical</u> — remember this when you're drawing them.

Most questions follow a set pattern...

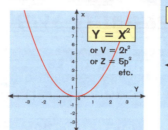

Y = X²
or V = 2r²
or Z = 5p²
etc.

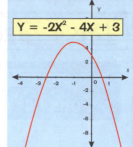

Y = -2X² - 4X + 3

---

1) Fill in the Table of Values

<u>Example</u>: "Fill in the table of values for the equation y = x² + 2x − 3 and draw the graph."

x	-5	-4	-3	-2	-1	0	1	2	3
y	12	5	0	-3	-4	-3	0	5	12

Work out each point <u>very carefully</u>, writing down all your working. Don't just plug it all straight in your calculator — you'll make mistakes. To check you're <u>doing it right</u>, make sure you can <u>reproduce</u> the y-values they've already given you.

2) Draw the Curve

1) <u>PLOT THE POINTS CAREFULLY</u>, and don't mix up the x and y values.

2) The points should form a <u>COMPLETELY SMOOTH CURVE</u>. If they don't, they're <u>wrong</u>.

<u>NEVER EVER</u> let one point drag your line off in some ridiculous direction. When a graph is generated from an equation, <u>you never get spikes or lumps</u> — only <u>MISTAKES</u>.

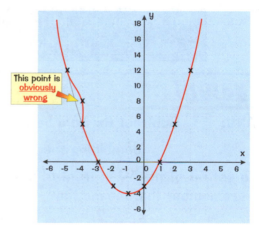

This point is <u>obviously wrong</u>

3) Use the Graph to Answer a Question

<u>Example</u>: "Use your graph to solve the equation x² + 2x − 3 = 0."

1) Look — the equation you've been asked to solve is what you get when you put <u>y=0</u> into the graph's equation, y = x² + 2x − 3.

2) To solve the equation, all you do is read the x-values where y = 0, i.e. where it crosses the x-axis.

3) So the solutions are <u>x = -3</u> and <u>x = +1</u>. (Quadratic eqns usually have 2 solutions.)

The Acid Test:

LEARN THE DETAILS of the method above for **DRAWING QUADRATIC GRAPHS** and **SOLVING THE EQUATION.**

Plot the graph of y = x² − x − 6 (use x-values from -4 to 5).
Use your graph to solve the equation x² − x − 6 = 0.

Inequalities

This is basically quite difficult, but it's still worth learning the easy bits in case they ask a very easy question on it, as well they might. Here are the easy bits:

The 4 Inequality Symbols:

> means "Greater than"   ≥ means "Greater than or equal to"
< means "Less than"   ≤ means "Less than or equal to"

REMEMBER, the one at the BIG end is BIGGEST

so "x > 4" and "4 < x" BOTH say: "x is greater than 4"

Algebra With Inequalities — this is generally a bit tricky

The thing to remember here is that inequalities are just like regular equations:

$$5x < x + 2$$
$$5x = x + 2$$

in the sense that all the normal rules for solving equations (See P.37) apply...

...BUT WITH ONE BIG EXCEPTION:

Whenever you MULTIPLY OR DIVIDE BY A NEGATIVE NUMBER, you must FLIP THE INEQUALITY SIGN.

Example: "Solve   5x < 6x + 2"

ANS: Subtract 6x from both sides: $5x - 6x < 2$

combining the x-terms gives: $-x < 2$

To get rid of the "−" in front of x you need to divide both sides by -1 — but remember that means the "<" has to be flipped as well, which gives:

$x > -2$ i.e. "x is greater than -2"   is the answer

(The < has flipped around into a >, because we divided by a −ve number)

This answer, x > −2, can be displayed as a shaded region on a number line like this:

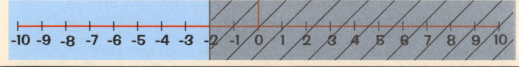

The main thing you should realise, is that MOST OF THE TIME you just treat the "<" or ">" as though it was an "=" and do all the usual algebra that you would for a regular equation. The "Big Exception" doesn't actually come up very often at all.

The Acid Test: LEARN: The 4 Inequality Signs, the similarity with EQUATIONS and the One Big Exception.

1) Solve this inequality: $4x + 3 \leq 6x + 7$.
2) Solve the inequalities and find the integer values of x which satisfy both:
   $2x + 9 \geq 1$ and $4x < 6 + x$

Trial and Improvement

This is a good method for finding approximate answers to equations that don't have simple whole number answers. Although it basically boils down to trial and error, there is a <u>clear method</u> which you must <u>learn</u> if you want to get it right...

Method

1) **<u>SUBSTITUTE TWO INITIAL VALUES</u>** into the equation that give **OPPOSITE CASES**.

Opposite cases means <u>one answer too big, one too small</u>. If they don't give opposite cases <u>try again</u>.

2) Choose your next value **IN BETWEEN** the previous two, and **PUT IT** into the equation.

<u>Continue the process</u>, choosing new values <u>between the two closest opposite cases</u>, (and preferably nearer to the one which is closer to the answer you want).

3) After only 3 or 4 steps you should have <u>2 NUMBERS</u> which are to the right degree of accuracy but **DIFFER BY 1 IN THE LAST DIGIT**.

E.g. if you had to get your answer to 2 DP, you'd eventually end up with say <u>5.43</u> and <u>5.44</u>, with these giving **OPPOSITE** cases.

4) Now take the **EXACT MIDDLE VALUE** to decide which is the answer you want.

E.g. for 5.43 and 5.44, you'd try 5.435 to see if the real answer was <u>between 5.43 and 5.435</u> or between <u>5.435 and 5.44</u>.

Example

"The equation $x^3 + x = 40$ has a solution between 3 and 3.5. Find this solution to 1 DP"

Try x = 3	$3^3 + 3 = 30$	(Too small)
Try x = 3.5	$3.5^3 + 3.5 = 46.375$	(Too big)

← (**2 opposite cases**)

40 is what we want and it's closer to 46.375 than it is to 30 so we'll choose our next value for x closer to 3.5 than 3.

Try x = 3.3	$3.3^3 + 3.3 = 39.237$	(Too small)

Good, this is very close, but we need to see if 3.4 is still too big or too small:

Try x = 3.4	$3.4^3 + 3.4 = 42.704$	(Too big)

Good, now we know that <u>the answer must be between 3.3 and 3.4</u>.
To find out which one it's nearest to, we have to try the <u>EXACT MIDDLE VALUE</u>: 3.35

Try x = 3.35	$3.35^3 + 3.35 = 40.945$ (Too big)

This tells us with certainty that the solution must be between 3.3 (too small) and 3.35 (too big), and so to 1 DP <u>it must round down to 3.3</u>. **ANSWER = 3.3**

The Acid Test:

"LEARN and TURN" — if you don't actually <u>commit it to memory</u>, then you've wasted your time even reading it.

To succeed with this method you must **<u>LEARN the 4 steps above</u>**. Do it now, and practise until you can <u>write them down without having to look back at them</u>. It's not as difficult as you think.

1) The equation $x^3 - 2x = 1$ has a solution between 1 and 2. Find it to 1 DP.

Angle Problems

Before you get stuck into this, have a look back at Page 14 from Module 6 on Parallel Lines. You could be tested on it so make sure you know it off by heart.

Angles and Circles

You need to know these two rules for geometry problems involving circles:

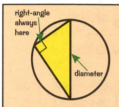

1) If a triangle has all its corners on a circle, and if its longest side is a diameter of the circle, the triangle will always be right-angled.

2) A tangent to a circle is perpendicular (at 90°) to the radius it meets on the edge of the circle.

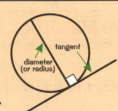

You're unlikely to be asked to recall these rules in the exam — what you'll probably have to do is use them to solve a geometry problem like this...

Example:

On the diagram shown, CE and FB are diameters. DG is a tangent. FB is parallel to EA. Use this diagram to find:
- a) angle x
- b) angle y
- c) angle z

Diagram not to scale

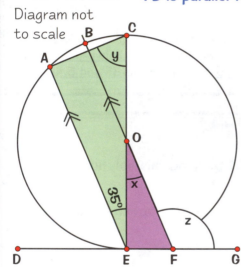

Don't worry if the overall diagram looks complicated. Just pay attention to the bits you need for that part of the question. A bit of practice and you're there...

a) Look at the angle AEC, it's 35°. There are also two parallel lines, so you can use "Alternate Angles" from p14 to tell you that: **x = 35°**

Angle ABC means the angle at B, formed by the two lines BA and BC.

b) To find y, we're dealing with the green triangle. From rule 1) above, angle EAC is 90°. And angles in a triangle add up to 180°. So: **y = 180 – 90 – 35 = 55°**

c) Now z is a bit of a tricky one. You need to see that z is a "Corresponding Angle" to angle AEG, i.e. it's the same. And from rule 2) above, angle OEG = 90°. So angle AEG = 35° + 90° = 125° which means: **z = AEG = 125°**

The Acid Test:

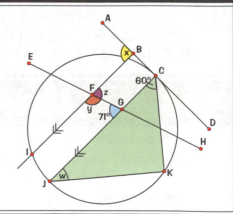

Now turn over and write down the two angle rules for circles.

1) Line CJ is a diameter. Line AD is a tangent. CJ is parallel to BI. Find angles w, x, y and z.

Pythagoras' Theorem

PYTHAGORAS' THEOREM is a handy little formula for **RIGHT-ANGLED TRIANGLES**. What it does is let you find the <u>length</u> of the <u>third side</u> when you know <u>two</u> of them.

The formula for Pythagoras' theorem is: $a^2 + b^2 = h^2$

where a and b are the <u>short sides</u> and h is the long side of the triangle (called the <u>hypotenuse</u>)

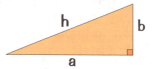

Remember that Pythagoras can only be used on **RIGHT-ANGLED TRIANGLES**.

The trouble is, the formula can be quite difficult to use. <u>Instead</u>, it's a lot better to just <u>remember</u> these <u>three simple steps</u>, which work every time:

1) **Square** *Them*
SQUARE THE TWO NUMBERS that you are given,
(use the x^2 button if you've got your calculator.)

2) **Add or Subtract**
To find the <u>longest side</u>, <u>ADD</u> the two squared numbers.
To find <u>a shorter side</u>, <u>SUBTRACT</u> the smaller one from the larger.

3) **Square Root**
Once you've got your answer, take the **SQUARE ROOT**.
(use the $\sqrt{}$ button on your calculator).

EXAMPLE 1: *"Find the missing side in the triangle shown."*

❶ <u>Square them</u>: $5^2 = 25$, $3^2 = 9$
❷ You want to find a <u>shorter side</u>, so **SUBTRACT**: $25 - 9 = 16$
❸ <u>Square root</u>: $\sqrt{16} = 4$

So the <u>missing side = 4m</u>

(You should always ask yourself: "Is it a *sensible answer*?" — in this case you can say "<u>YES</u>, because it's shorter than 5m, as it should be since 5m is the longest side, but not too much shorter")

5m, 3m, ?

EXAMPLE 2: *"Find the missing side in the triangle shown."*

❶ <u>Square them</u>: $5^2 = 25$, $12^2 = 144$
❷ You want to find the <u>longest side</u>, so **ADD**: $25 + 144 = 169$
❸ <u>Square root</u>: $\sqrt{169} = 13$

So the <u>missing side = 13m</u>

(You should always ask yourself: "Is it a *sensible answer*?" — in this case you can say YES, because it's longer than both the other sides, but not too much longer — like 50 or something daft like that!)

?, 5m, 12m

The Acid Test: LEARN the <u>3 steps</u> of the Pythag. method.

Now <u>turn over and write down what you've learned</u>.

1) Then apply the above method to find the missing side BC:
2) Another triangle has sides of 7 m, 24 m and 25 m.
   Is it a right-angled triangle? How do you know?

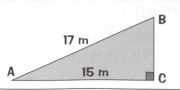

17 m, 15 m, A, B, C

Volume and Converting Measures

Volume of a *Prism*

Hopefully you already know the <u>very easy formula</u> for volume of a cuboid. If not, look at p16 now! For this module you need to do <u>prisms</u>, which are marginally more exciting.

> <u>A PRISM</u> is a solid (3-D) object which has a <u>CONSTANT AREA OF CROSS-SECTION</u> — i.e. it's the same shape all the way through.

Triangular Prism

Constant Area of Cross-section

Length

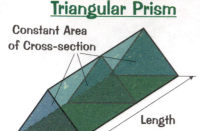

Hexagonal Prism
(a flat one, certainly, but still a prism)

Length

Constant Area of Cross-section

Circular Prism
(or Cylinder)

Constant Area of Cross-section

Length

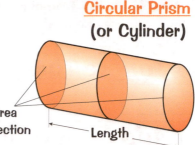

> $$\text{Volume of prism} = \text{Cross-sectional Area} \times \text{length}$$

> $$V = A \times l$$

As you can see, the formula for the volume of a prism is <u>very simple</u>. The <u>difficult</u> part, usually, is <u>finding the area of the cross-section</u>.

Converting Area and Volume Measurements

> $1m^2 = 100cm \times 100cm = 10,000cm^2$

1) To change area measurements from m^2 to cm^2 multiply the area in m^2 by 10,000 (e.g. $3m^2 = 30,000cm^2$).

2) To change area measurements from cm^2 to m^2 divide the area in cm^2 by 10,000 (e.g. $45,000cm^2 = 4.5m^2$).

$1m^2$

100cm

← 100cm →

> $1m^3 = 100cm \times 100cm \times 100cm = 1,000,000cm^3$

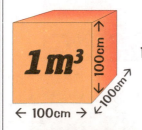

$1m^3$

100cm

100cm

← 100cm →

1) To change volume measurements from m^3 to cm^3 multiply the volume in m^3 by 1,000,000 (e.g. $3m^3 = 3,000,000cm^3$).

2) To change volume measurements from cm^3 to m^3 divide the volume in cm^3 by 1,000,000 (e.g. $4,500,000cm^3 = 4.5m^3$).

The Acid Test:

<u>LEARN</u> this page. Then turn over and try to write it all down. <u>Keep trying until you can do it.</u>

1) Find the volume of these prisms:

2) Convert these measurements:
    a) 23 m² → cm²   b) 34,500 cm² → m²
    c) 5.2m³ → cm³   d) 100,000 cm³ → m³

a)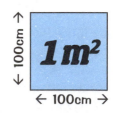

4cm
3cm
7cm
9cm

b)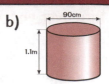

90cm
1.1m

Coordinates

Finding the Coordinates of a Midpoint

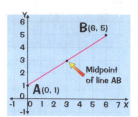

1) The MIDPOINT OF A LINE SEGMENT is just the point that's right bang in the middle of it (no trick questions here).

2) The only thing you really need to know about midpoints is how to find the coordinates of one.

3) And it's pretty easy. The x-coordinate of the midpoint is the average of the x-coordinates of the end points — and the same goes for the y-coordinates.

EXAMPLE: "A and B have coordinates (2,1) and (6,3). Find the midpoint of the line AB."

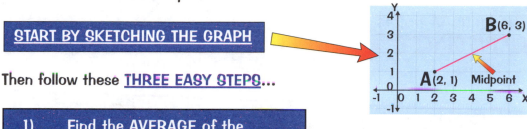

START BY SKETCHING THE GRAPH

Then follow these **THREE EASY STEPS...**

1) Find the AVERAGE of the X-COORDINATES of the two points.

Average of x-coordinates = (2+6) ÷ 2 = 4

2) Find the AVERAGE of the Y-COORDINATES of the two points.

Average of y-coordinates = (1+3) ÷ 2 = 2

3) Plonk them IN BRACKETS.

Plonk them in brackets (x-coordinate first): (4, 2)

Z Coordinates are for 3-D space

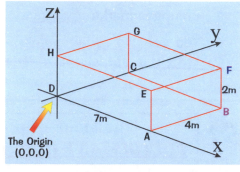

1) All z-coordinates do is extend the normal x-y coordinates into a third direction, z, so that all positions then have 3 coordinates: (x,y,z)

2) This means you can give the coordinates of the corners of a box or any other 3-D SHAPE.

For example in this drawing, the coordinates of B and F are   B(7,4,0)   F(7,4,2)

The Acid Test:

Learn the 3 easy steps for finding midpoints. Close the book and write them down.

Plot these points on some graph paper: A(1,4), B(5,6), C(3,2), D(7,0).

1) Draw a line between points A and B and find the midpoint of the line AB.
2) Draw a line between points C and D and find the midpoint of line CD.

Look at the 3-D graph above.
3) Write down the coordinates of points A, C and E.

Loci and Constructions

A <u>LOCUS</u> (another ridiculous maths word) is simply:

A PATH that shows <u>all the points which fit in with a given rule</u>

Make sure you <u>learn</u> how to do these <u>PROPERLY</u> using a <u>RULER AND COMPASSES</u> as shown.

1) The locus of points which are "*A FIXED DISTANCE from a given POINT*"

This locus is simply a <u>CIRCLE</u>.

Pair of Compasses

A given point

The LOCUS of points a fixed distance from it

2) The locus of points which are "*A FIXED DISTANCE from a given LINE*"

This locus is an <u>OVAL SHAPE</u>

It has <u>straight sides</u> (drawn with a <u>ruler</u>) and <u>ends</u> which are <u>perfect semicircles</u> (drawn with <u>compasses</u>).

Semicircle ends drawn with compasses

A given line

The LOCUS of points a fixed distance from it

3) The locus of points which are "*EQUIDISTANT from TWO GIVEN LINES*"

Equidistant just means "the same distance".

1) Keep the compass setting <u>THE SAME</u> while you make <u>all four marks</u>.

2) Make sure you <u>leave</u> your compass marks <u>showing</u>.

3) You get <u>two equal angles</u> — i.e. this LOCUS is actually an <u>ANGLE BISECTOR</u>.

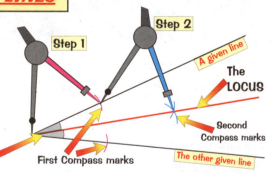

Step 1

Step 2

A given line

The LOCUS

Second Compass marks

The other given line

First Compass marks

4) The locus of points which are "*EQUIDISTANT from TWO GIVEN POINTS*"

(In the diagram below, A and B are the two given points)

Step 1

Step 3

The LOCUS

Step 1

A

Step 2

B

Step 2

<u>This LOCUS</u> is all the points which are the <u>same distance</u> from A and B.

This time the locus is actually the <u>PERPENDICULAR BISECTOR</u> of the line joining the two points.

Loci and Constructions

Constructing accurate 60° angles

1) They may well ask you to draw an <u>accurate 60° angle</u>.

2) One place they're needed is for drawing an <u>equilateral triangle</u>.

3) Make sure you <u>follow the method</u> shown in this diagram, and that you can do it <u>entirely from memory</u>.

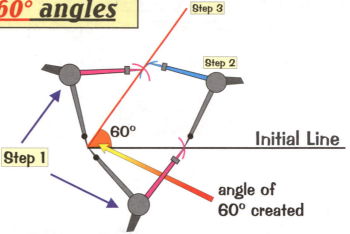

Step 3

Step 2

Step 1

60°

Initial Line

angle of 60° created

Constructing accurate 90° angles

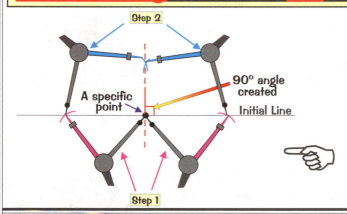

Step 2

A specific point

90° angle created

Initial Line

Step 1

1) They might want you to draw an <u>accurate 90° angle</u>.

2) They won't accept it just done "<u>by eye</u>" or with a ruler — if you want to get the marks, you've got to do it <u>the proper way</u> with <u>compasses</u> like I've shown you here.

3) Make sure you can <u>follow the method</u> shown in this diagram.

Drawing the **Perpendicular** from a **Point** to a **Line**

1) This is similar to the one above but <u>not quite</u> the same — make sure you can do <u>both</u>.

2) Again, they won't accept it just done "<u>by eye</u>" or with a ruler — you've got to do it the <u>proper way</u> with <u>compasses</u>.

3) <u>Learn</u> the diagram.

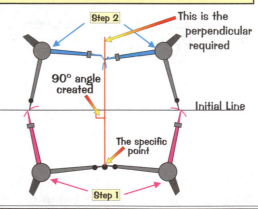

Step 2

This is the perpendicular required

90° angle created

Initial Line

The specific point

Step 1

The Acid Test: LEARN EVERYTHING ON THESE TWO PAGES

Now cover up these two pages and draw an example of each of the four loci. Also draw an equilateral triangle and a square, both with fabulously accurate 60° and 90° angles. Also, draw a line and a point and construct the perpendicular from the point to the line.

Formula Triangles

Formula triangles are <u>extremely useful tools</u> for lots of tricky maths problems. They're <u>very easy to use</u> and <u>very easy to remember</u>. Watch:

If 3 things are related by a formula that looks either

like this: $A = B \times C$ or like this: $B = \dfrac{A}{C}$

then you can put them into a <u>FORMULA TRIANGLE</u> like this:

1) First decide where the letters go:

1) If there are <u>TWO LETTERS MULTIPLIED TOGETHER</u> in the formula then they must go <u>ON THE BOTTOM</u> of the Formula Triangle (and so <u>the other one</u> must go <u>on the top</u>).

For example the formula "<u>F = m×a</u>" fits into
a formula triangle like this →

2) If there's <u>ONE THING DIVIDED BY ANOTHER</u> in the formula then the one <u>ON TOP OF THE DIVISION</u> goes <u>ON TOP IN THE FORMULA TRIANGLE</u> (and so the other two must go <u>on the bottom</u> — it doesn't matter which way round).

So the formula "<u>Speed = Distance / Time</u>" fits into a formula triangle like this ↑.

2) Using the Formula Triangle:

Once you've got the formula triangle sorted out, the rest is easy:

1) <u>COVER UP the thing you want to find</u> and just <u>WRITE DOWN what's left showing</u>.
2) <u>PUT IN THE VALUES</u> for the other two things and just <u>WORK IT OUT</u>.

<u>EXAMPLE:</u>

"Using <u>F = m×a</u>, find the value of 'a' when F = 20 and m = 50"

<u>ANSWER:</u> Using the formula triangle, we want to find "a" so we cover "a" up, and that leaves "F/m" showing (i.e. F÷m).
So "a = F/m", and putting the numbers in we get: a = 20/50 = <u>0.4</u>

The Acid Test:
<u>LEARN THIS WHOLE PAGE</u> then turn over and <u>write down</u> all the important details including the examples.

Speed and Density

You might think this is physics, but density is mentioned in the maths syllabus.
The standard formula for density is:

Density = Mass ÷ Volume

so we can put it in a FORMULA TRIANGLE like this:

One way or another you <u>must remember</u> this formula for density, because they won't
give it to you.   The best method by far is to remember the <u>order of the letters</u> in the
formula triangle as D^MV or <u>DiMoV</u> (The Russian Agent!).

EXAMPLE: Find the volume of an object which has
a mass of 40 g and a density of 6.4 g/cm³

ANSWER: To find volume, <u>cover up V</u> in the formula triangle.
This leaves M/D showing,   so V = M ÷ D
$$= 40 \div 6.4$$
$$= \underline{6.25 \text{ cm}^3}$$

Speed = Distance ÷ Time

This is very common. In fact it probably comes up every single year — and they never
give you the formula!   Either <u>learn it beforehand</u> or wave goodbye to <u>lots of easy marks</u>.
Life isn't all bad though — there's an easy FORMULA TRIANGLE:

Of course you still have to <u>remember the order of the letters</u> in the
triangle (S^DT) — but this time we have the word <u>SoDiT</u> to help you.

So if it's a question on speed, distance and time just say: <u>SOD IT</u>.

EXAMPLE: "A car travels 90 miles at 36 miles per hour. How long does it take?"

ANSWER: <u>We want to find the TIME</u>, so <u>cover up T</u> in the triangle which leaves D/S,

so   T = D/S   = Distance ÷ speed = 90÷36 = <u>2.5 hours</u>

**LEARN THE <u>FORMULA TRIANGLE</u>, AND YOU'LL FIND QUESTIONS
ON SPEED, DISTANCE AND TIME <u>VERY EASY</u>.**

The Acid Test: LEARN the formulas for <u>DENSITY</u> and <u>SPEED</u>
— and also the two <u>Formula triangles</u>.

1) What's the formula for Density?
2) A metal object has a volume of 45 cm³ and a mass of 743 g. What is its density?
3) Another piece of the same metal has a volume of 36.5 cm³. What is its mass?
4) What's the formula for speed, distance and time?
5) Find the time taken, for a person walking at 3.2 km/h to cover 24 km.
   Also, find how far she'll walk in 3 hrs 30 mins.

Probability — Relative Frequency

Before you start this page, look over all the probability stuff from Module 6 on pages 21-2. Sometimes you <u>can't calculate the probability of something happening exactly</u> — you need to use <u>relative frequency</u>. And this isn't the number of times your granny comes to visit...

Fair or Biased?

The probability of rolling a three on a dice is $\frac{1}{6}$ — you know that each of the 6 numbers on a dice is <u>equally likely</u> to be rolled, and there's <u>only 1 three</u>.

BUT this only works if it's a <u>fair dice</u>. If the dice is a bit <u>wonky</u> (the technical term is "<u>biased</u>") then each number <u>won't</u> have an equal chance of being rolled. That's where <u>Relative Frequency</u> comes in — you can use it to work out probabilities when things might be wonky.

Do the Experiment Again and Again and Again and Again

You need to do an experiment <u>over and over again</u> and then do a quick calculation. (Remember, an experiment could just mean rolling a dice.)
Usually the results of these experiments will be written in a <u>table</u>.

The Formula for Relative Frequency

$$\text{Probability of something happening} = \frac{\text{Number of times it has happened}}{\text{Number of times you tried}}$$

You can work out the relative frequency as a <u>fraction</u> but usually <u>decimals</u> are best.

The important thing to remember is:

> The more times you do the experiment, the more accurate the probability will be.

Example:

Number of Times the dice was rolled	10	20	50	100
Number of threes rolled	2	5	11	36
Relative frequency	$\frac{2}{10}=0.2$	$\frac{5}{20}=0.25$	$\frac{11}{50}=0.22$	$\frac{36}{100}=0.36$

So, what's the probability? We've got <u>4 possible answers</u>, but the best is the one worked out using the <u>highest number of dice rolls</u>.
This makes the probability of rolling a three on this dice <u>0.36</u>.

And since for a fair, unbiased dice, the probability of rolling a three is $\frac{1}{6}$ (about 0.17), then our dice <u>is probably biased</u>.

The Acid Test

1) A 3-sided spinner is spun 100 times – it lands on red 43 times, blue 24 times and green the other times. Calculate the relative frequency of each outcome.

Grouped Frequency Tables

Before you start this page, have a read through p25 from module 6 on frequency tables. This page shows some examples of frequency tables where the data is put into groups.

Example 1:

The marks of 28 students in a test (out of 80) were:

63, 45, 44, 52, 58,
49, 48, 22, 37, 34,
44, 49, 66, 73, 69,
32, 49, 29, 55, 57,
30, 72, 59, 46, 70,
39, 27, 40

As a Grouped Table

Marks	Tally	Frequency
$0 \leq x \leq 10$		
$11 \leq x \leq 20$		
$21 \leq x \leq 30$	||||	4
$31 \leq x \leq 40$	||||	5
$41 \leq x \leq 50$	|||| |||	8
$51 \leq x \leq 60$	||||	5
$61 \leq x \leq 70$	||||	4
$71 \leq x \leq 80$	||	2
Total		28

Example 2:

The weights (in kg) of a bunch of 20 school kids are shown below.

67.3, 45.6, 47.7, 65.0,
54.2, 76.5, 44.6, 34.3,
69.8, 53.9, 32.3, 54.5,
78.9, 59.8, 57.4, 30.0,
79.1, 46.2, 66.0, 51.6

As a Grouped Table

Weight w (kg)	Tally	Frequency
$30 \leq w < 40$	|||	3
$40 \leq w < 50$	||||	4
$50 \leq w < 60$	|||| |	6
$60 \leq w < 70$	||||	4
$70 \leq w < 80$	|||	3
Total		20

Reading the Intervals

In the top table, "$0 \leq x \leq 10$" means x is either between 0 and 10 or it is one of those values.

In the bottom table, "$30 \leq w < 40$" means w is between 30 and 40 or it could equal 30, but it can't equal 40 (40 would go in the next group).

The intervals used in the top table are suitable for whole number data (note that you couldn't place 30.5 on this table — it would fall in between two groups). Whole numbers are an example of discrete data — data that can only take certain values.

The intervals in the bottom table are suitable for any numbers (30.5, 50.9999) because there are no gaps between the groups. Data like this that can take any values within a range is called continuous data.

The Acid Test

1) Say if the following are continuous or discrete data and design a data table for each one:
   a) shoe size of 20 adults   b) height of 30 adults

Grouped Frequency Tables

Forgotten what mode and mean mean? You'd better flick back to page 23 before doing this.

Estimating The Mean For Grouped Data

You need to be able to estimate the mean for data in a grouped frequency table.
Note you can only <u>estimate</u> the mean because you don't know the <u>actual values</u>.

The method is a bit fiddly at first, but it's easy once you've learnt it:

1) <u>Add a 3rd row</u> and enter <u>MID-INTERVAL VALUES</u> for each group.
2) <u>Add a 4th row</u> and <u>multiply FREQUENCY × MID-INTERVAL VALUE</u> for each group.
3) Work out the <u>TOTALS</u> of rows 2 and 4.
4) Get the mean by dividing <u>ROW 4 TOTAL</u> by <u>ROW 2 TOTAL</u>.

*Note — if your table is arranged like the ones on the previous page,
you'll need to add extra columns rather than rows...*

Example:

The table below shows the distribution of weights of 60 children.
Find the modal group and estimate the mean.

Weight (kg)	$30 \leq w < 40$	$40 \leq w < 50$	$50 \leq w < 60$	$60 \leq w < 70$	$70 \leq w < 80$
Frequency	8	16	18	12	6

The modal group is just the one with the highest frequency: $50 \leq w < 60$ kg

To find the mean, add two rows to the table as described above:

Weight (kg)	$30 \leq w < 40$	$40 \leq w < 50$	$50 \leq w < 60$	$60 \leq w < 70$	$70 \leq w < 80$	TOTALS
Frequency	8	16	18	12	6	60
Mid-Interval Value	35	45	55	65	75	—
Frequency × Mid-Interval Value	280	720	990	780	450	3220

Now, just divide the totals to get an estimate of the mean:

$$\text{Mean} = \frac{\text{Overall Total (Final Row)}}{\text{Frequency Total (2nd Row)}} = \frac{3220}{60} = \underline{53.7}$$

The Acid Test:

<u>LEARN</u> all the details on this page, then <u>turn over</u> and
<u>write down everything you've learned</u>. Good, clean fun.

1) Estimate the mean for this table:
2) State the modal group.

Length L (cm)	$15.5 \leq L < 16.5$	$16.5 \leq L < 17.5$	$17.5 \leq L < 18.5$	$18.5 \leq L < 19.5$
Frequency	12	18	23	8

Revision Summary for Module Seven

It's almost time for your favourite bit — the end of module questions. But before you start these, you need to read the following pages from module 6. These are needed for Module 7 too.

- Multiplying and Dividing with Decimals (p2-4)
- Area and Circumference of Circles (p15)
- Surface Area and Nets (p17)
- Scatter Graphs (p24)

OK, I'll let you do the questions now...

1) What are the six rules for dealing with powers? Why is "x² = 9... x = 3" only half the story?

2) To find the cube root of 125, what should you say to yourself?

3) What are the two rules for estimating a calculation?

4) What are the four handy rules for multiplying / dividing numbers greater / less than 1?

5) Which calculator button can you use to simplify ratios?

6) What is the formula triangle for ratios? What are two rules for using it?

7) What are the three steps of the method of proportional division?

8) Write down the meanings of "percent" and "OF". How would you work out 40% of 79kg?

9) What is a prime number? Explain exactly what LCM and HCF mean.

10) Describe the "mildly entertaining" factor tree method.

11) What does stating the rule to extend a number pattern actually boil down to?

12) What's the formula for the nth term of a "common difference" number sequence?

13) Make formulas out of the following text: a) To find y, take x away from 7, then divide it all by 3. b) A floodlight uses £1 of electricity to warm up, then uses £2 of electricity per hour to run. Write a formula for C, the total cost in £ of using the floodlight for h hours.

14) Write down the 3 step method for solving equations.

15) Write down both methods of multiplying out two brackets such as $(x - 4)(x - 1)$.

16) What shape do quadratic graphs always have?

17) Explain what the four inequality symbols mean, and state the main difference between inequalities and regular equations when you're trying to solve them.

18) Write down the Trial and Improvement method.

19) If a triangle has all its corners on a circle, and its longest side is a diameter, what type is it?

20) What can you say about a tangent to a circle and the radius it meets?

21) Write down a formula and draw a labelled triangle to explain Pythagoras' Theorem. This theorem ONLY works on one type of triangle. What is it?

22) Detail the three step method for using Pythagoras' Theorem.

23) What is a prism? What are the formulas for volume of a cuboid and a prism.

24) Write down the three easy steps in calculating the coordinates of a midpoint.

25) What is a "Locus"? Draw four examples of different types of locus and write what they are.

26) Construct an accurate 60° and 90° angle using compasses, then draw a perpendicular from a point to a line. Check your drawings using a protractor.

27) What are the two types of formula that can be put into a formula triangle?

28) What are the formula triangles for density and for speed?

29) What is the formula for relative frequency?

30) Explain what discrete and continuous data are. What does $40 \leq x \leq 45$ mean?

31) Describe the method for estimating the mean of grouped data.

Standard Index Form

Standard Form and Standard Index Form are the same thing.
So remember both of these names as well as what it actually is:

Ordinary Number: 4,300,000   In Standard Form: 4.3×10^6

Standard form is really useful for writing very big or very small numbers in a more convenient way, e.g.

56,000,000,000 would be 5.6×10^{10} in standard form.
0.000 000 003 45 would be 3.45×10^{-9} in standard form.

but ANY NUMBER can be written in standard form and you need to know how to do it:

What it Actually is:

A number written in standard form must ALWAYS be in EXACTLY this form:

$$A \times 10^n$$

This number must always be BETWEEN 1 AND 10.

(The fancy way of saying this is:

"$1 \leqslant A < 10$" — they sometimes write that in Exam questions — don't let it put you off, just remember what it means).

This number is just the NUMBER OF PLACES the Decimal Point moves.

Learn The Three Rules:

1) The front number must always be BETWEEN 1 AND 10

2) The power of 10, n, is purely: HOW FAR THE D.P. MOVES

3) n is +ve for BIG numbers,   n is −ve for SMALL numbers
   (This is much better than rules based on which way the D.P. moves.)

Examples:

1) "Express 35 600 in standard form".

METHOD:
1) Move the D.P. until 35 600 becomes 3.56 ("$1 \leqslant A < 10$")
2) The D.P. has moved 4 places so n=4, giving: 10^4
3) 35600 is a BIG number so n is +4, not −4

ANSWER:
$3.5600. = \underline{3.56 \times 10^4}$

2) "Express 8.14×10^{-3} as an ordinary number".

METHOD:
1) 10^{-3}, tells us that the D.P. must move 3 places...
2) ...and the "−" sign tells us to move the D.P. to make it a SMALL number. (i.e. 0.00814, rather than 8140)

ANSWER:
$8.14 = \underline{0.00814}$

Standard Index Form

Standard Form and The Calculator

People usually manage all that stuff about moving the decimal point OK (apart from always forgetting that FOR A BIG NUMBER it's "ten to the power +ve something" and FOR A SMALL NUMBER it's "ten to the power –ve something"), but when it comes to doing standard form on a calculator it's often a sorry saga of confusion and mistakes...

But it's not so bad really — you just have to learn it, that's all...

1) Entering Standard Form Numbers EXP

The button you MUST USE to put standard form numbers into the calculator is the EXP (or EE) button — but DON'T go pressing X 10 as well, like a lot of people do, because that makes it WRONG.

EXAMPLE: "Enter 2.67 × 10^{15} into the calculator"

Just press: 2.67 EXP 15 =   and the display will be   2.67 ^{15}

Note that you ONLY PRESS the EXP (or EE) button — you DON'T press X or 10 at all.

2) Reading Standard Form Numbers:

The big thing you have to remember when you write any standard form number from the calculator display is to put in the "×10" bit. Some calculators will display a little "×10", but others don't. If yours doesn't, you have to remember to add it in.

EXAMPLE: "Write down the number   7.986 ^{05} as a finished answer."

As a finished answer this must be written as 7.986 × 10^5.

It is NOT 7.986^5 so DON'T write it down like that — it'll be completely wrong.

The Acid Test:
LEARN the Three Rules and the Two Calculator Methods, then turn over and write them down.

Now cover up these 2 pages and answer these:
1) What are the Three Rules for standard form?
2) Express 958,000 in standard index form.   3) And the same for 0.00018
4) Express 4.56 × 10^3 as an ordinary number.
5) Work this out using your calculator: 3.2 × 10^{12} ÷ 1.6 × 10^{-9} , and write down the answer, first in standard form and then as an ordinary number.

Percentage problems

Take a peek back at page 32 from module 7 before doing this page.

This page shows you how to handle <u>four different types</u> of percentage question.
Learn these and you'll be able to handle anything the examiners <u>throw at you</u>...

Type 1   "Find x% of y" — e.g. Find 15% of £46 $\Rightarrow$ 0.15 × 46 = <u>£6.90</u>

Type 2   "Express x as a percentage of y"
e.g. Give 40p as a percentage of £3.34 $\Rightarrow$ (40 ÷ 334) × 100 = <u>12%</u>

Type 3   — IDENTIFIED BY <u>NOT</u> GIVING THE "<u>ORIGINAL VALUE</u>"

These are the type most people get wrong – but only because they don't recognise them as a type 3 and don't apply this simple method:

Example: | A house increases in value by 20% to £72,000.
Find what it was worth <u>before</u> the rise.

Method:

$$£72,000 = 120\%$$
$$\div 120 \searrow$$
$$£600 = 1\%$$
$$\times 100 \searrow$$
$$£60,000 = 100\%$$

So the original price was <u>£60,000</u>

An <u>INCREASE</u> of 20% means that £72,000 represents <u>120% of the original</u> value. If it was a **DROP** of 20%, then we would put "£72,000 = <u>80%</u>" instead, and then divide by 80 on the LHS, instead of 120.

Always set them out <u>exactly like this example</u>. The trickiest bit is deciding the top % figure on the RHS — the 2nd and 3rd rows are <u>always</u> 1% and 100%.

Type 4 — Repeated Percentage Problems

"Ali buys a really big potato for £800. The value of her potato depreciates by 25% each year. Find the value of Ali's potato after 3 years."

Value after 1 year is: £800 × 0.75 = £600
Value after 2 years is: £600 × 0.75 = £450
Value after 3 years is: £450 × 0.75 = £337.50

A loss of 25% means you need to work out 100 – 25 = 75% of the original value. 75% as a decimal is 0.75.

So you're basically just multiplying by 0.75 for <u>each year</u>. A quicker way of <u>setting this out</u> would be: £800 × 0.75 × 0.75 × 0.75, or even better: <u>£800 × 0.75³</u>.
If you had to work out the potato's value in say, 58 years, you'd <u>have</u> to do it this way!
Have a look forward to p93 of module ten where this method is covered in detail.

The Acid Test:
LEARN the details for TYPE 3 and TYPE 4 QUESTIONS, then <u>turn over and write it all down</u>.

1) A trader buys watches for £5 and sells them for £7. Find his profit as a percentage.
2) A car depreciates by 30% to £14,350. What was it worth before?
3) Find the value after 4 years of an Emu that cost £30 and loses 10% value per year.

Basic Algebra

This page covers some of the basic algebra techniques you need to know for this module.

Multiplying out Brackets

1) The thing <u>outside</u> the brackets multiplies <u>each separate term</u> inside the brackets.
2) When letters are <u>multiplied together</u>, they are just written <u>next to each other</u>, pq.
3) Remember, $R \times R = R^2$, and TY^2 means $T \times Y \times Y$, whilst $(TY)^2$ means $T \times T \times Y \times Y$.
4) Remember a minus outside the bracket <u>REVERSES ALL THE SIGNS</u> when you multiply.

1) $3(2x + 5) = $ <u>$6x + 15$</u>   2) $4p(3r - 2t) = $ <u>$12pr - 8pt$</u>

3) $-4(3p^2 - 7q^3) = -12p^2 + 28q^3$ (note both signs have been reversed — Rule 4)

<u>DOUBLE BRACKETS</u> — you get <u>4 terms</u>, and usually 2 of them combine to leave <u>3 terms</u>.

$$(2P - 4)(3P + 1) = (2P \times 3P) + (2P \times 1) + (-4 \times 3P) + (-4 \times 1)$$
$$= 6P^2 + 2P - 12P - 4$$
$$= \underline{6P^2 - 10P - 4} \quad \text{(these 2 combine)}$$

<u>SQUARED BRACKETS</u> — Always write these out as <u>TWO BRACKETS</u>:

E.g. $(3d + 5)^2$ should be written out as $(3d + 5)(3d + 5)$ and then worked out as above. You should always get <u>FOUR TERMS</u> from a pair of brackets.

The usual <u>WRONG ANSWER</u> is: $(3d + 5)^2 = 9d^2 + 25$ (Eeek!)
The <u>CORRECT ANSWER</u> is:

$(3d + 5)^2 = (3d + 5)(3d + 5) = 9d^2 + 15d + 15d + 25 = \underline{9d^2 + 30d + 25}$

D.O.T.S. — The Difference Of Two Squares:

$$a^2 - b^2 = (a + b)(a - b)$$

The "difference of two squares" (D.O.T.S. for short) is where you have "one thing squared" take away "another thing squared". Too many people have more trouble than they should with this, probably because they don't make enough effort to learn it as a separate item in its own right. Best learn it now, eh, before it's too late.

1) Factorise $9P^2 - 16Q^2$.   Answer: $9P^2 - 16Q^2 = (3P + 4Q)(3P - 4Q)$

2) Factorise $1 - T^4$.   Answer: $1 - T^4 = (1 + T^2)(1 - T^2)$

3) Solve $x^2 - 36 = 0$ by factorising.   Answer: Using D.O.T.S., $x^2 - 36 = (x + 6)(x - 6) = 0$
So $(x + 6) = 0$ or $(x - 6) = 0$, $x = $ – 6 or 6

OK, so you could have said: $x^2 = 36$, $x = +6, -6$. But factorising shows you where the +ve and –ve answers come from...

The Acid Test:

<u>LEARN</u> the methods for multiplying out the <u>three types of brackets</u> and learn the <u>D.O.T.S.</u> rule.

1) Multiply these out: a) $5x(x - 3)$ b) $(3x - 1)(2x + 4)$ c) $(2x + 6)^2$

Solving Equations

Have a look back at page 37 of module seven which shows the basic techniques for solving equations and rearranging formulas. Now the trouble is, when the equations start getting complicated, it gets harder to work out what to do and gets easier to make mistakes. So to help, here is a step-by-step method for solving equations which will work every time. Just carry out all the steps in order and the answer will simply pop out.

To illustrate the sequence of steps we'll use this equation:

$$\sqrt{2 - \frac{x+4}{2x+5}} = 3$$

The Six Steps Applied to Equations

1) Get rid of any square root signs by squaring both sides:

$$2 - \frac{x+4}{2x+5} = 9$$

2) Get everything off the bottom by cross-multiplying up to EVERY OTHER TERM:

$$2 - \frac{x+4}{2x+5} = 9 \quad \Rightarrow \quad 2(2x+5) - (x+4) = 9(2x+5)$$

3) Multiply out any brackets:

$$4x + 10 - x - 4 = 18x + 45$$

4) Collect all subject terms on one side of the "=" and all non-subject terms on the other. Remember to reverse the +/− sign of any term that crosses the "="

+18x moves across the "=" and becomes -18x
+10 moves across the "=" and becomes -10
-4 moves across the "=" and becomes +4

$$4x - x - 18x = 45 - 10 + 4$$

5) Combine together like terms on each side of the equation, and reduce it to the form "Ax = B", where A and B are just numbers (or bunches of letters, in the case of formulas):

$$-15x = 39$$

("Ax = B":
A = -15, B = 39,
x is the subject)

6) Finally slide the A underneath the B to give "x = B/A", divide, and that's your answer.

$$x = \frac{39}{-15} = -2.6$$

So x = -2.6

The Seventh Step (if you Need It)

If the term you're trying to find is squared, don't panic.

Follow steps 1) to 6) like normal, but solve it for x^2 instead of x:

$$x^2 = 9$$
$$x = \pm 3$$

7) Take the square root of both sides and stick a ± sign in front of the expression on the right:

Don't forget the ± sign...
(P.28 if you don't know what I mean).

The Acid Test:
LEARN the 7 STEPS for solving equations and rearranging formulas. Turn over and write them down.

1) Solve these equations: a) $5(x + 2) = 8 + 4(5 - x)$ b) $\frac{4}{x+3} = \frac{6}{4-x}$ c) $x^2 - 21 = 3(5 - x^2)$

Rearranging Formulas

Rearranging formulas means making one letter the subject, e.g. getting "y= " from something like $2x + z = 3(y + 2p)$.

Generally speaking "solving equations" is easier, but just remember this:

1) EXACTLY THE SAME METHOD APPLIES TO BOTH FORMULAS AND EQUATIONS.
2) THE SAME SEQUENCE OF STEPS APPLIES EVERY TIME.

We'll illustrate this by making "y" the subject of this formula: $M = \sqrt{2K - \dfrac{K^2}{2y + 1}}$

The Six Steps Applied to Formulas

1) Get rid of any square root signs by squaring both sides: $\qquad M^2 = 2K - \dfrac{K^2}{2y + 1}$

2) Get everything off the bottom by cross-multiplying up to EVERY OTHER TERM:

$$M^2 = 2K - \frac{K^2}{2y + 1} \quad \Rightarrow \quad M^2(2y + 1) = 2K(2y + 1) - K^2$$

3) Multiply out any brackets: $\qquad 2yM^2 + M^2 = 4Ky + 2K - K^2$

4) Collect all subject terms on one side of the "=" and all non-subject terms on the other. Remember to reverse the +/- sign of any term that crosses the "=".

$+4Ky$ moves across the "=" and becomes $-4Ky$
$+M^2$ moves across the "=" and becomes $-M^2$

$$2yM^2 - 4Ky = -M^2 + 2K - K^2$$

5) Combine together like terms on each side of the equation, and reduce it to the form "Ax = B", where A and B are just bunches of letters which DON'T include the subject (y). Note that the LHS has to be FACTORISED:

$$(2M^2 - 4K)y = 2K - K^2 - M^2$$

("Ax = B" i.e. $A = (2M^2 - 4K)$, $B = 2K - K^2 - M^2$, y is the subject)

6) Finally slide the A underneath the B to give "$x = \dfrac{B}{A}$", (cancel if possible) and that's your answer. $\qquad$ So $\qquad y = \dfrac{2K - K^2 - M^2}{(2M^2 - 4K)}$

The Seventh Step (if you Need It)

$M = \sqrt{2K - \dfrac{K^2}{2y^2 + 1}}$

If the term you're trying to make the subject of the equation is squared, this is what you do:

Follow steps 1) to 6), $\quad y^2 = \dfrac{2K - K^2 - M^2}{(2M^2 - 4K)}$ $\quad$ (I've skipped steps 1) - 6) because they're exactly the same as the first example — but with y^2 instead of y.)

and then...

7) Take the square root of both sides and stick a ± sign in front of the expression on the right: $\quad y = \pm\sqrt{\dfrac{2K - K^2 - M^2}{(2M^2 - 4K)}}$ $\quad$ Remember — square roots can be +ve or –ve. See P.28.

The Acid Test:
LEARN the 7 STEPS for solving equations and rearranging formulas. Turn over and write them down.

1) Rearrange "$F = \frac{9}{5}C + 32$" from "F= ", to "C= " and then back the other way.

2) Make p the subject of these: $\quad$ a) $\dfrac{p}{p + y} = 4$ $\qquad$ b) $\dfrac{1}{p} = \dfrac{1}{q} + \dfrac{1}{r}$ $\qquad$ c) $\dfrac{1}{p^2} = \dfrac{1}{q} + \dfrac{1}{r}$

Simultaneous Equations

Simultaneous equations are <u>two equations</u> with <u>two unknowns</u> (e.g. x and y).

For example $y = x + 3$ and $x + y = 6$.

To <u>solve them</u> you need to find a value for <u>x and for y</u> for which <u>both equations</u> are true. As with quadratic equations, there are several ways to solve them, but the method you need to know for this module is <u>elimination</u>. It's called this because you basically have to "eliminate" one of the unknowns to end up with a "normal" equation in only <u>1 unknown</u>.

Six Steps For Simultaneous Equations

We'll use these two equations for our example: $2x = 6 - 4y$ and $-3 - 3y = 4x$

1) <u>Rearrange both equations</u> into the form <u>ax + by = c</u> where a, b, c are numbers (which can be negative).   Also label the two equations   —① and   —②

$$2x + 4y = 6 \quad —①$$
$$-4x - 3y = 3 \quad —②$$

2) You need to <u>match up the numbers in front</u> (the "coefficients") of either the x's or y's in both equations. To do this you may need to multiply one or both equations by a suitable number. You should then relabel them: —③ and   —④

①×2 : $4x + 8y = 12 \quad — ③$
$$-4x - 3y = 3 \quad — ④$$

3) <u>Add or subtract</u> the two equations to <u>eliminate</u> the terms with the same coefficient. If the <u>coefficients are the same</u> (both +ve or both −ve) then <u>SUBTRACT</u>. If the <u>coefficients are opposite</u> (one +ve and one −ve) then <u>ADD</u>.

③ + ④ $0x + 5y = 15$

4) <u>Solve</u> the resulting equation to find whichever letter is left in it.

$$5y = 15 \Rightarrow \underline{y = 3}$$

5) <u>Substitute</u> this value back into equation ① and solve it to find the other quantity.

Sub in ①: $2x + 4×3 = 6 \Rightarrow 2x + 12 = 6 \Rightarrow 2x = -6 \Rightarrow \underline{x = -3}$

6) Then substitute both these values into equation ② to <u>make sure it works</u>. If it doesn't then you've done something wrong and you'll have to do it all again.

Sub x and y in ② : $-4×-3 - 3×3 = 12 - 9 = \underline{3}$, which is right, so it's worked.
So the solutions are: $\underline{x = -3}$, $\underline{y = 3}$

The Acid Test:
LEARN the 6 Steps for solving Simultaneous Equations by Elimination.

1) Remember, you only know them when you can write them all out from memory, so turn over the page and see if you can write down all six steps. Then try again.
2) Apply the six steps to find F and G when:
   $2F - 10 = 4G$ and $3G = 4F - 15$

Simultaneous Equations with Graphs

You've just seen a <u>marginally painful</u> algebra method for solving two simultaneous equations. Well for some light relief (and also because you have to know it), here is another way to think about simultaneous equations:

> The simultaneous equations we just solved, $2x = 6 - 4y$ and $-3 - 3y = 4x$, are both <u>STRAIGHT LINE EQUATIONS</u>. The solutions we found, $x=-3$ and $y=3$, are actually the single point (-3, 3) where these <u>TWO LINES MEET</u>.

This gives us a nice <u>graphical method</u> to solve simultaneous equations...

Solving *Simultaneous Equations* Using Graphs

> The solution of two simultaneous equations is simply the x and y values <u>where their graphs cross</u>.

Three Step <u>Method</u>

1) Do a <u>"TABLE OF VALUES"</u> for both equations.

2) Draw the two <u>GRAPHS</u>.

3) Find the x- and y-values <u>WHERE THEY CROSS</u>.

Easy Peasy.

Example

"Draw the graphs for "$y = 2x + 3$" and "$y = 6 - 4x$" and then use your graphs to solve these simultaneous equations."

1) <u>TABLE OF VALUES</u>
   for both equations:

X	-2	0	2
Y	-1	3	7

X	0	1	2
Y	6	2	-2

2) <u>DRAW THE GRAPHS</u>:

3) <u>WHERE THEY CROSS</u>, x = ½, y = 4.

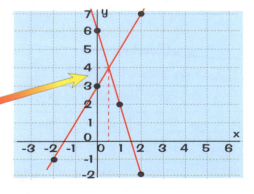

And that's the answer: <u>x = ½ and y = 4</u>

(You can stick these values back into the original equations to prove they're right.)

The Acid Test:

<u>LEARN</u> the Simple Rule and the <u>3 step method</u> for <u>solving simultaneous equations</u> using <u>GRAPHS</u>.

1) Cover the page and write down the Simple Rule and the 3 step method.
2) Use graphs to find the solutions to these pairs of equations:
   a) $y = 4x - 4$ and $y = 6 - x$ b) $y = 2x$ and $y = 6 - 2x$

Quadratic Equations

There are several ways to solve quadratic equations and if you ask me, they're all truly wonderful. Sadly, for this module you only need to know the factorising method...

Solving a Quadratic by Factorisation

"Factorising a quadratic" means "putting it into 2 brackets".

The standard format for quadratic equations is: $ax^2 + bx + c = 0$
In this module you'll only be given quadratics with $a = 1$
such as "$x^2 + 3x + 2 = 0$", which makes them easier.

For questions where 'a' isn't 1, see page 82 of module 9.

Factorising Method When a = 1

1) **ALWAYS** rearrange into the **STANDARD FORMAT**: $ax^2 + bx + c = 0$

2) Write down the **TWO BRACKETS** with the x's in: (x   )(x   )=0

3) Then find 2 numbers that **MULTIPLY to give "c"** (the end number)
   but also **ADD/SUBTRACT to give "b"** (the coefficient of x)

4) Put them in and check that the +/− signs work out properly.

EXAMPLE: "Solve $x^2 - x = 12$ by factorising."

ANSWER: 1) First rearrange it (into the standard format): $x^2 - x - 12 = 0$

2) a = 1, so the initial brackets are (as ever):   (x   )(x   ) = 0

3) We now want to look at all pairs of numbers that multiply to give c (=12),
   but which also add or subtract to give the value of b:

1×12	Add/subtract to give:	13 or 11
2×6	Add/subtract to give:	8 or 4 this is what we're
3×4	Add/subtract to give:	7 or ① ← after (=±b)

4) So 3 and 4 will give b = ±1, so put them in: (x   3)(x   4)=0

5) Now fill in the +/− signs so that the 3 and 4 add/subtract to give -1 (=b),
   Clearly it must be +3 and −4 so we'll have: (x + 3)(x − 4)=0

6) As an **ESSENTIAL check, EXPAND the brackets** out again to make sure they
   give the original equation: $(x + 3)(x - 4) = x^2 + 3x - 4x - 12 = \underline{x^2 - x - 12}$

We're not finished yet mind, because $(x + 3)(x - 4) = 0$ is only the factorised form of the equation — we have yet to give the actual **SOLUTIONS**. This is very easy:

7) **THE SOLUTIONS** are simply the two numbers in the brackets, but with **OPPOSITE +/− SIGNS**: i.e. $x = -3$ or $+4$

> Make sure you remember that last step. It's the difference between **SOLVING THE EQUATION** and merely factorising it.

The Acid Test: LEARN the 7 steps for solving quadratics when a=1.

1) Solve by factorising: a) $x^2 + 5x - 24 = 0$ b) $x^2 - 6x + 9 = 16$

Graphical Inequalities

Before reading this page, have a good read through p40 of module 7 which shows you how to handle basic inequalities — you need to know it for module 8 too. Done that? Good.

Now, this page shows you how to handle questions with <u>more than one inequality</u>. These questions are always done by <u>drawing graphs</u> and <u>shading regions</u>.

Method

> 1) <u>CONVERT each INEQUALITY to an EQUATION</u>
>   by simply putting an "=" in place of the "<" or ">"
> 2) <u>DRAW THE GRAPH FOR EACH EQUATION</u>
> 3) <u>Work out WHICH SIDE of each line you want</u>
>   Put x=0 and y=0 into the inequality to see if the <u>ORIGIN</u> is on the correct side.
> 4) <u>SHADE THE REGION</u> this gives you

Example

"Shade the region represented by:
$x + y < 5$, $y > x + 2$ and $y > 1$"

1) <u>CONVERT EACH INEQUALITY TO AN EQUATION</u>:
The inequalities become $x + y = 5$, $y = x + 2$ and $y = 1$

2) <u>DRAW THE GRAPH FOR EACH EQUATION</u> (see p12 or p65)

3) <u>WORK OUT WHICH SIDE OF EACH LINE YOU WANT</u>
This is the fiddly bit. Substitute $x = 0$ and $y = 0$ (the origin) into each inequality and see if this makes the inequality <u>true</u> or <u>false</u>.

<u>In $x + y < 5$:</u>
$x = 0$, $y = 0$ gives $0 < 5$ which is <u>true</u>.
This means the <u>origin</u> is on the <u>correct</u> side of the line.

<u>In $y > x + 2$:</u>
$x = 0$, $y = 0$ gives $0 > 2$ which is <u>false</u>.
So the origin is on the <u>wrong side</u> of this line.

<u>In $y > 1$:</u>
$x = 0$, $y = 0$ gives $0 > 1$ which is <u>false</u>.
So the origin is on the <u>wrong side</u> of this line too.

4) <u>SHADE THE REGION</u>
You want the region that satisfies all of these:
– below $x + y = 5$ (because the origin <u>is</u> on this side)
– above $y = x + 2$ (because the origin <u>isn't</u> on this side)
– above $y = 1$ (because the origin <u>isn't</u> on this side).

The Acid Test:

LEARN the <u>Four Steps</u> for doing <u>graphical inequalities</u>, then <u>turn over</u> and <u>write them down</u>.

1) Show on a graph the region described by the following three conditions:
$x + y < 6$, $y > 0.5$, $y < 2x - 2$

Straight Lines

Any straight line graph can be described by a simple equation.
You should be able to <u>recognise</u> a lot of graphs just from their <u>equations</u>.

1) <u>Horizontal</u> and <u>Vertical</u> lines: "x = a" and "y = a"

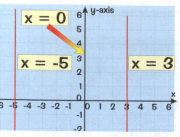

<u>x = a</u> is a <u>vertical line</u>
<u>through "a"</u> on the x-axis

<u>y = a</u> is a <u>horizontal line</u>
<u>through "a"</u> on the y-axis ☞

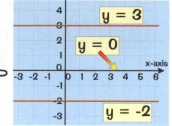

Don't forget: <u>the y-axis is also the line x=0</u>

Don't forget: <u>the x-axis is also the line y=0</u>

2) <u>The</u> <u>Main Diagonals</u>: "<u>y = x</u>" and "<u>y = –x</u>"

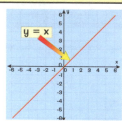

"<u>y = x</u>" is the <u>main diagonal</u> that
goes <u>UPHILL</u> from left to right.

"<u>y = -x</u>" is the <u>main diagonal</u> that
goes <u>DOWNHILL</u> from left to right. ☞

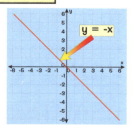

3) Other <u>Sloping Lines</u> Through the origin:
"<u>y = ax</u>" and "<u>y = –ax</u>"

<u>y = ax</u> and <u>y = -ax</u> are the equations for
<u>A SLOPING LINE THROUGH THE ORIGIN.</u>

The value of "<u>a</u>" (known as the <u>gradient</u>) tells you the
steepness of the line. The bigger "a" is, the steeper the
slope. A <u>MINUS SIGN</u> tells you it slopes <u>DOWNHILL</u>.

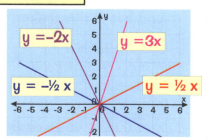

<u>All Other</u> <u>Straight</u> Lines

Other straight-line equations are a little more complicated, but there is an easy way to
identify them. Remember: All straight-line equations just contain "<u>something x,</u>
<u>something y, and a number</u>".

<u>Straight lines:</u>		<u>NOT straight lines:</u>	
$x - y = 0$	$y = 2 + 3x$	$y = x^3 + 3$	$2y - 1/x = 7$
$2y - 4x = 7$	$4x - 3 = 5y$	$1/y + 1/x = 2$	$x(3 - 2y) = 3$
$3y + 3x = 12$	$6y - x - 7 = 0$	$x^2 = 4 - y$	$xy + 3 = 0$

The Acid Test:

<u>LEARN</u> all the specific graphs on this page and
also how to <u>identify straight-line equations.</u>

Now turn over the page and write down everything you've learned.

Straight Lines

So all straight-line equations contain "<u>something x, something y, and a number</u>".
Once you've identified a straight-line equation, you can draw its graph.

1) Drawing a *Straight Line* Using the "x = 0", "y = 0" Method

> 1) <u>Set x=0</u> in the equation, and <u>find y</u> — this is where it <u>crosses the y-axis</u>.
>
> 2) <u>Set y=0</u> in the equation and <u>find x</u> — this is where it <u>crosses the x-axis</u>.
>
> 3) <u>Plot these two points</u> and <u>join them up with a straight line</u>.

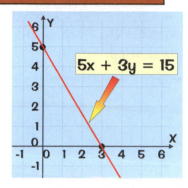

EXAMPLE: "Draw the graph of $5x + 3y = 15$"

1) Putting <u>x = 0</u> gives "$3y = 15$" $\Rightarrow$ <u>y = 5</u>

2) Putting <u>y = 0</u> gives "$5x = 15$" $\Rightarrow$ <u>x = 3</u>

3) So plot <u>(0, 5)</u> and <u>(3, 0)</u> on the graph
and join them up with a straight line:

Only doing 2 points is risky unless you're sure the equation is definitely a straight line — but then that's the big thrill of living life on the edge, isn't it.

2) Drawing a *Straight Line* using y = mx + c

All straight-line equations can be written in the form <u>y = mx + c</u>,
where — "<u>m</u>" equals the <u>gradient</u> (steepness) of the line.
      — "<u>c</u>" is the "<u>y-intercept</u>" (where the graph hits the y-axis).

If the equation isn't already in this form, then the first thing you have to do is <u>rearrange</u> it.
Then you can <u>draw the graph</u> using the method below.

1) Get the equation into the form "<u>y = mx + c</u>". → E.g. $2y - 4x = 7 \rightarrow y = 2x + 3\frac{1}{2}$ (m=2, c=3½)

2) <u>Put a dot on the y-axis</u> at the value of c. → This is the y-intercept.

3) Then go <u>along one unit</u> and <u>up or down by the value of m</u> and make another dot.

4) <u>Repeat</u> the same "step" in <u>both directions</u>.

5) Finally check that the gradient <u>looks right</u>.

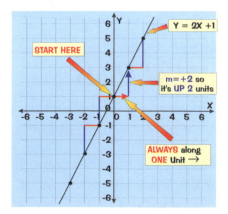

EXAMPLE — Draw the graph of the equation $y = 2x + 1$.
1) The equation is in the correct form, so you can go on to step 2).
2) "c" = 1, so put a first dot at y = 1 on the y-axis.
3) Go along 1 unit → and then up by 2 because "m" = +2.
4) Repeat the same step, 1→ 2↑ in both directions.
5) CHECK: a gradient of <u>+2</u> should be <u>quite steep</u> and <u>uphill</u> left to right which it is, so it looks OK.

The Acid Test:

LEARN the <u>two methods</u> for drawing graphs of straight-line equations, then turn over and write them down.

1) Sketch these graphs: a) $y = 2 + x$ b) $y = x + 6$ c) $4x - 2y = 0$ d) $y = 1 - \frac{1}{2}x$
    e) $x = 2y + 4$ f) $2x - 6y - 8 = 0$ g) $0.4x - 0.2y = 0.5$ h) $y = 3 - x + 2$

Straight Lines

Gradient, remember, is a measure of the <u>steepness</u> of a line. If it's <u>positive</u>, the line slopes <u>upwards</u>, if it's <u>negative</u>, it slopes <u>downwards</u>. If it's <u>zero</u>, it's just a <u>horizontal line</u>.

Finding the Gradient

1) Find TWO ACCURATE POINTS and COMPLETE THE TRIANGLE

Both points should be in the <u>upper right quadrant</u> if possible (to keep all the numbers positive).

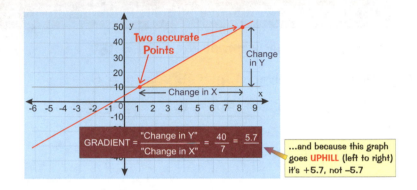

GRADIENT = $\dfrac{\text{"Change in Y"}}{\text{"Change in X"}}$ = $\dfrac{40}{7}$ = 5.7

...and because this graph goes **UPHILL** (left to right) it's +5.7, not –5.7

2) Find the CHANGE IN Y and the CHANGE IN X

Make sure you subtract the x coords. the <u>same way round</u> as you do the y coords. E.g. y coord. of pt A – y coord. of pt B <u>and</u> x coord of pt A – x coord of pt B.

3) LEARN this formula, and use it:

$$\text{GRADIENT} = \frac{\text{CHANGE IN Y}}{\text{CHANGE IN X}}$$

4) Check the SIGN'S right.

If it slopes <u>UPHILL</u> left → right (⬈) <u>then it's positive</u>
If it slopes <u>DOWNHILL</u> left → right (⬂) <u>then it's negative</u>

If you subtracted the coordinates the right way round, the sign should be correct. If it's not, go back and check what you've done.

Parallel Lines

1) Remember — the general equation of a straight line is <u>y = mx + c</u>, where <u>m</u> is the <u>gradient</u> and c is the y-intercept.

2) Parallel lines have the <u>same value of m</u>, i.e. the <u>same gradient</u>. So the lines: y = 2x + 3, y = 2x and y = 2x – 4 are all parallel.

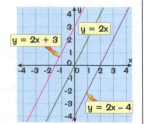

The Acid Test:

LEARN the FOUR STEPS for finding a gradient then <u>turn over</u> and <u>WRITE THEM DOWN</u> from memory.

1) Plot these 3 points on a graph: (0,3) (2,0) (5,-4.5) and then join them up with a straight line. Now carefully apply the FOUR STEPS to find the gradient of the line.

More Graphs

If you're beginning to think that there's nothing more to life than straight-line graphs, you'd better think again. There are <u>two more types</u> of graphs you need to be able to recognise and plot — <u>cubics</u> (x^3 graphs) and <u>reciprocals</u> ($1/x$ graphs).

1) x^3 Graphs:

y = "something with x^3 in it"

All x^3 graphs have the same basic <u>wiggle</u> in the middle, but it can be a flat wiggle or a more pronounced wiggle.

Notice that "<u>-x^3 graphs</u>" always come <u>down from top left</u> whereas the <u>+x^3</u> ones go <u>up from bottom left</u>.

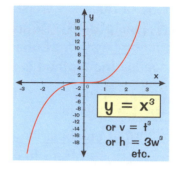

$$y = x^3$$
or $v = t^3$
or $h = 3w^3$
etc.

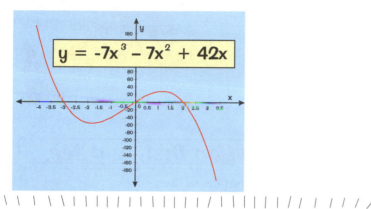

$$y = -7x^3 - 7x^2 + 42x$$

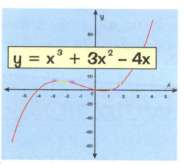

$$y = x^3 + 3x^2 - 4x$$

To plot a cubic or reciprocal graph, use the table of values method — see Module 7 page 39 on quadratic graphs. If you've learnt the shapes of these graphs, you'll be able to check that yours looks about right.

2) $1/x$ Graphs:

$y = \dfrac{A}{x}$, where A is some number

These graphs are <u>all the same shape</u>, the only difference being how close in they get at the corner. They are all <u>symmetrical about the line $y=x$</u>. This is also the graph you get when x and y are in <u>inverse proportion</u>.

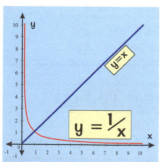

$y = x$

$$y = \frac{1}{x}$$

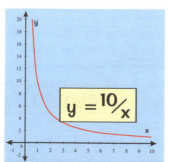

$$y = \frac{10}{x}$$

The Acid Test:

LEARN all the details about the <u>2 Types of Graph</u>, their equations and their shapes.

Then <u>turn over</u> and <u>sketch three examples</u> of each of the <u>two types</u> of graph — and if you can also give some extra details about their equations, <u>so much the better</u>. Remember, if you don't <u>LEARN IT</u>, then it's a waste of time even reading it. This is true for all revision.

Combinations of Transformations

Before you start this page look back at pages 18 and 19 from module 6 to learn how to do all these transformations individually. Then get your teeth stuck into this beast of a page...

The Better You Know Them All — The Easier it is

These kinds of question aren't so bad — but ONLY if you've LEARNT the four transformations really well (see p18-19). If you don't know them, then you certainly won't do too well at spotting a combination of one followed by another.
That's because the method is basically "Try it and see..."

Example

"What combination of two transformations takes you from triangle A to triangle B?"

(There's usually a few different ways of getting from one shape to the other — but remember you only need to find ONE of them.)

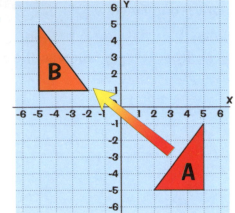

Method: Try an obvious transformation first, and See...

If you think about it, the answer can only be a combination of two of the four types shown on the last page, so you can immediately start to narrow it down:

1) Since the shapes are the same size we can rule out enlargements.
2) Next, try a reflection (in either the x-axis or the y-axis).
   Here we've tried a reflection in the y-axis, to give shape A':
3) You should now easily be able to see the final step
   from A' to B — it's a translation of $\begin{pmatrix} 0 \\ 6 \end{pmatrix}$.

And that's it DONE — from A to B is simply a combination of:

A REFLECTION IN THE Y-AXIS followed by a TRANSLATION OF $\begin{pmatrix} 0 \\ 6 \end{pmatrix}$

At least that's one answer anyway. If instead we decided to reflect it in the x-axis first (as shown here) then we'd get another answer (see Acid Test below) — but both are right.

"But which transformation do I try first?" I hear you cry

Well it just depends on how it looks. The more transformation questions you do, the more obvious that first guess becomes. You know what that means — practice practice practice...

The Acid Test: LEARN the main points on this page.
Then cover it up and write them all down.

1) What pair of transformations will convert shape C into shape D?
   What pair will convert shape D to shape C?
2) In the example above, find the other transformation needed to
   get to shape B after reflecting shape A in the x-axis.

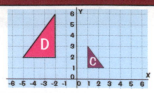

Enlargements and Dimensional Analysis

There Are Four Key Features To Enlargements

1) If the scale factor is bigger than 1 the shape gets bigger.

A to B is an Enlargement, Scale Factor 1½

2) If the scale factor is smaller than 1 (i.e. a fraction like ½) then the shape gets smaller. (Really this is a reduction, but you still call it an enlargement, scale factor ½)

A to B is an Enlargement of Scale Factor ½

3) If the scale factor is negative then the shape pops out the other side of the enlargement centre. If the scale factor is -1, it's exactly the same as a rotation of 180°.

A to B is an enlargement of scale factor -2.
B to A is an enlargement of scale factor -½.

4) The scale factor also tells you the relative distance of old points and new points from the centre of enlargement — this is very useful for drawing an enlargement, because you can use it to trace out the positions of the new points:

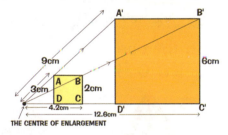

9cm
3cm
2cm
6cm
4.2cm
12.6cm
THE CENTRE OF ENLARGEMENT

Identifying Formulas Just by Looking at Them

The posh name for this is dimensional analysis, and concerns only three things:

LENGTH, AREA and VOLUME

In formulas of course, lengths are represented by letters, so when you look at a formula you're looking for: groups of letters multiplied together in ones, twos or threes.

But remember, π is not a length.

There are three key rules which you must know:

AREA FORMULAS always have LENGTHS MULTIPLIED IN PAIRS

VOLUME FORMULAS always have LENGTHS MULTIPLIED IN GROUPS OF THREE

LENGTH FORMULAS (such as perimeter) always have LENGTHS OCCURRING SINGLY

Examples:

r^2 means r × r, don't forget

$4\pi r^2 + 6d^2$ (area)	$Lwh + 6r^2L$ (volume)
$4\pi r + 15L$ (length)	$6hp + \pi r^2 + 7h^2$ (area)
$3p(2b + a)$ (area)	$3\pi h(L^2 + 4P^2)$ (volume)

Watch out for tricky ones with brackets — you should multiply out the brackets first (see p.57).

The Acid Test:

1) Draw the triangle A(2,1) B(5,2) C(4,4) and enlarge it by a scale factor of -1.5, centre the origin. Label the new triangle A' B' C' and give the coordinates of its corners.

2) Identify each of these expressions as an area, volume, or perimeter:

πr^2 Lwh πd $\frac{1}{2}bh$ $2bh + 4lh$ $4r^2h + 3\pi d^3$ $2\pi r(3L + 5T)$

Trigonometry

There are several methods for doing Trig and they're all pretty much the same. However, the method shown below has a number of advantages, mainly because the formula triangles mean the same method is used every time, (no matter which side or angle is being asked for). *Using formula triangles is covered on p48, by the way.*

Method

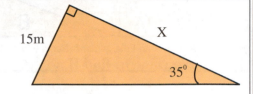

1) Label the three sides O, A and H (Opposite, Adjacent and Hypotenuse).

2) Write down from memory "SOH CAH TOA". (Sounds like a Chinese word, "Sockatoa!")

3) Decide which two sides are involved: O,H   A,H   or   O,A and select SOH, CAH or TOA accordingly.

4) Turn the one you choose into a FORMULA TRIANGLE:

S O H   C A H   T O A

5) Cover up the thing you want to find (with your finger), and write down whatever is left showing.

6) Translate into numbers and work it out.

7) Finally, check that your answer is sensible.

Some Nitty Gritty Details

1) The Hypotenuse is the LONGEST SIDE. The Opposite is the side OPPOSITE the angle being used (θ), and the Adjacent is the (other) side NEXT TO the angle being used.

2) In the formula triangles, Sθ represents SIN θ, Cθ is COS θ, and Tθ is TAN θ.

3) Remember, TO FIND THE ANGLE — USE INVERSE. i.e. press **INV** or **SHIFT** or **2nd**, followed by SIN, COS or TAN (and make sure your calculator is in DEG mode).

4) You can only use SIN, COS and TAN on RIGHT-ANGLED TRIANGLES — you may have to add lines to the diagram to create one, especially with isosceles triangles.

The Acid Test:
LEARN the 7 Steps of the Method and the Four Nitty Gritty Details. Then turn over and write them down.

Practising past paper questions is very important, but the whole point of doing so is to check and consolidate the methods you have already learnt. Don't make the mistake of thinking it's pointless learning these 7 steps. If you don't know them all thoroughly, you'll just keep on getting questions wrong.

Trigonometry

Example 1: "Find x in the triangle shown."

1) Label O, A, H
2) Write down "SOH CAH TOA"
3) Two sides involved: O, H

4) So use

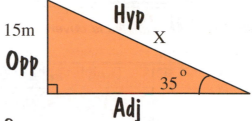

5) We want to find H so cover it up to leave: $H = \dfrac{O}{s\theta}$

6) Translate: $x = \dfrac{15}{\sin 35}$

Press `15` `÷` `SIN` `35` `=` `26.151702` **So ans = 26.2m**

7) Check it's sensible: yes it's about twice as big as 15, as the diagram suggests.

Example 2: "Find the angle θ in this triangle."

Note the usual way of dealing with an ISOSCELES TRIANGLE: split it down the middle to get a RIGHT ANGLE:

1) Label O, A, H
2) Write down "SOH CAH TOA'"
3) Two sides involved: A, H

4) So use

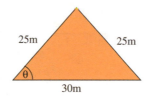

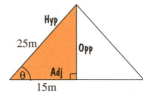

5) We want to find θ so cover up Cθ to leave: $C\theta = \dfrac{A}{H}$

6) Translate: $\cos\theta = \dfrac{15}{25} = 0.6$

NOW USE INVERSE: $\theta = $ INV COS (0.6)

Press `INV` `COS` `0.6` `=` `53.130102` **So ans. = 53.1°**

7) Finally, is it sensible? — Yes, the angle looks like about 50°.

Angles of Elevation And Depression

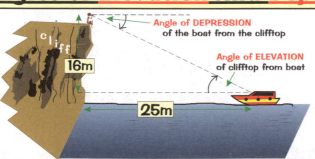

Angle of DEPRESSION of the boat from the clifftop

Angle of ELEVATION of clifftop from boat

1) The Angle of Depression is the angle downwards from the horizontal.
2) The Angle of Elevation is the angle upwards from the horizontal.
3) The Angles of Elevation and Depression are EQUAL.

The Acid Test: Practise these three questions until you can apply the method fluently and without having to refer to it at all.

1) Find x
2) Find θ

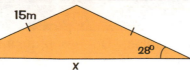

3) Calculate the angles of elevation and depression in the boat drawing above.

Probability — Tree Diagrams

Before working your way through this forest of tree diagrams, you might want a reminder of how to calculate probabilities. *If so, it's covered on pages 21-22 of Module 6.*

General Tree Diagram

Tree diagrams are all pretty much the same, so it's a pretty darned good idea to learn these basic details (which apply to **ALL** tree diagrams) — ready for the one in the Exam.

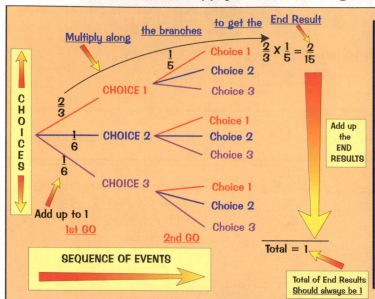

1) Always **MULTIPLY ALONG THE BRANCHES** (as shown) to get the **END RESULTS.**

2) **On any set of branches which all meet at a point**, the numbers must always **ADD UP TO 1.**

3) Check that your diagram is **correct** by **making sure the End Results ADD UP TO ONE.**

4) To answer any question, simply **ADD UP THE RELEVANT END RESULTS** (see below).

A likely Tree Diagram Question

EXAMPLE: "A box contains 5 red disks and 3 green disks. One disk is taken at random. The disk is then **replaced** in the box and a second disk is taken. Draw a tree diagram and hence find the probability that **both disks are the same colour.**"

The first disk is taken and then put back in the box. This means that the probabilities for the 2nd disk are *unaffected* by whatever the first disk was — there are still 5 red disks and 3 green disks to choose from. So the picks are *independent*.

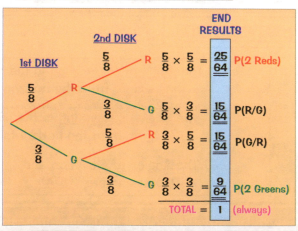

Once the tree diagram is drawn all you then need to do to answer the question is simply **select the RELEVANT END RESULTS** and then **ADD THEM TOGETHER:**

2 REDS   (25/64)
2 GREENS   (9/64)

$$\frac{25}{64} + \frac{9}{64} = \frac{34}{64} = \frac{17}{32}$$

The Acid Test:

LEARN the **GENERAL TREE DIAGRAM** and the **4 points** that go with it.

1) A bag contains 6 red tarantulas and 4 black tarantulas. One girl plucks out a tarantula at random, then puts it back in the bag. Another girl then does the same. Draw a tree diagram to find the probability that they get different coloured ones.

Probability — Tree Diagrams

Four Extra Details for the Tree Diagram method:

1) Always break up the question INTO A SEQUENCE OF SEPARATE EVENTS.

E.g. "3 coins are tossed together" — just split it into 3 separate events.
You need this sequence of events to be able to draw any sort of tree diagram.

2) DON'T FEEL you have to draw COMPLETE tree diagrams.

Learn to adapt them to what is required.
E.g. "What is the chance of throwing a dice 3 times and
getting 2 sixes followed by an even number?"
This diagram is all you need to get the answer: $\frac{1}{6} \times \frac{1}{6} \times \frac{1}{2} = \frac{1}{72}$

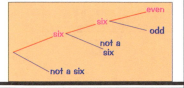

3) WATCH OUT for DEPENDENT PROBABILITIES...

...where the fraction on each branch depends on what happened on the previous
branch, e.g. bags of sweets, packs of cards etc, where the bottom number of the
fractions also changes as items are removed. E.g. $\frac{11}{25}$ then $\frac{10}{24}$ etc.

4) With "AT LEAST" questions, it's always (1 – Prob of "the other outcome"):

For example, "Find the probability of having AT LEAST one girl in 4 children."
There are in fact 15 different ways of having "AT LEAST one girl in 4 children" which
would take a long time to work out, even with a tree diagram.

The clever trick you should know is this:
The prob of "AT LEAST something or other" is just (1 – prob of "the other outcome")
which in this case is (1 – prob of "all 4 boys") = (1 – 1/16) = 15/16.

Example

"Herbert has two spare tickets for Royal Ascot. His two chums and
five doting aunties all want a ticket, so Herbert puts their names in a hat and picks out
two at random. Find the probability that Herbert's chums each get a ticket."

Easy peasy if you draw this tree diagram:

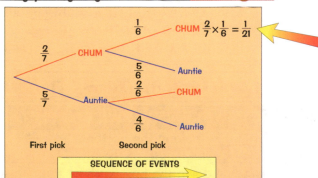

So the answer is 1/21.

These probabilities are dependent — the
fractions on the second branch are affected by
what happens on the first branch. If Herbert's
first pick is a chum, the remaining 6 people will
consist of 1 chum and 5 aunties. If he picks an
auntie first, there will still be 2 chums but only 4
aunties left to choose from.

The Acid Test:

LEARN THE WHOLE OF THIS PAGE. Then turn over and
write down all the key points and the example too.

1) Paul and his friends play a board game every Monday and Thursday. They have a choice of
three types of game on each day. They choose a logic game with probability 0.3, a skill
game with probability 0.2 or a luck game with probability 0.5. Assuming their choices are
independent, find the probability that at least one of this week's two games is a logic game.

Cumulative Frequency

FOUR KEY POINTS

1) **CUMULATIVE FREQUENCY** just means **ADDING IT UP AS YOU GO ALONG**.
2) You have to **ADD A THIRD ROW** to the table — the **RUNNING TOTAL** of the 2nd row.
3) **When plotting the graph**, always plot points **using the HIGHEST VALUE in each group** (of row 1) with the value from **row 3**.   i.e. plot 13 at **160**, etc. (see below).
4) Cumulative Frequency is always plotted **up the side** of a graph, not across.

Example

Height (cm)	$140 \le x < 150$	$150 \le x < 160$	$160 \le x < 170$	$170 \le x < 180$	$180 \le x < 190$	$190 \le x < 200$	$200 \le x < 210$
Frequency	4	9	20	33	36	15	3
Cumulative Frequency	4 (AT 150)	13 (AT 160)	33 (AT 170)	66 (AT 180)	102 (AT 190)	117 (AT 200)	120 (AT 210)

The graph is plotted from these pairs: (150, 4) (160, 13) (170, 33) (180, 66) etc.

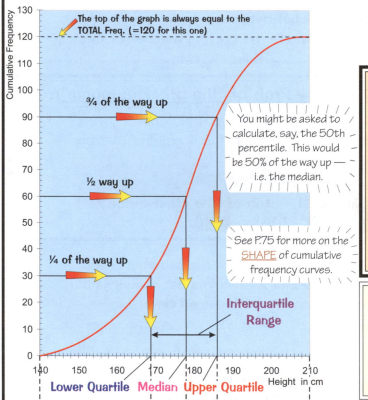

The top of the graph is always equal to the TOTAL Freq. (=120 for this one)

¾ of the way up

½ way up

¼ of the way up

Interquartile Range

Lower Quartile Median Upper Quartile

You might be asked to calculate, say, the 50th percentile. This would be 50% of the way up — i.e. the median.

See P.75 for more on the SHAPE of cumulative frequency curves.

For a cumulative frequency curve there are **THREE VITAL STATISTICS** which you need to know how to find:

1) **MEDIAN**
Exactly halfway UP, then across, then down and **read off the bottom scale**.

2) **LOWER AND UPPER QUARTILES**
Exactly ¼ and ¾ UP the side, then across, then down and **read off the bottom scale**.

3) **THE INTERQUARTILE RANGE**
The distance **on the bottom scale** between the lower and upper quartiles.

So from the cumulative frequency curve for this data, we get these results:

MEDIAN = 178cm
LOWER QUARTILE = 169cm
UPPER QUARTILE = 186cm
INTERQUARTILE RANGE = 17cm (186-169)

A Box Plot shows the Inter-Quartile Range as a Box

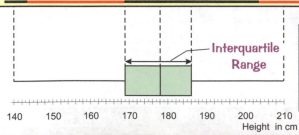

Interquartile Range

TO CREATE YOUR VERY OWN BOX PLOT:
1) Draw the scale along the bottom.
2) Draw a box the length of the interquartile range.
3) Draw a line down the box to show the median.
4) Draw "whiskers" up to the maximum and minimum.

(They're sometimes called "Box and Whisker diagrams".)

The Acid Test: LEARN THIS PAGE, then cover it up and do these:

1) **Complete** this cumulative frequency table:
2) **Draw the graph**. Find the **3 Vital Statistics**.
3) Draw a box plot under the graph.

No of fish	41 – 45	46 – 50	51 – 55	56 – 60	61 – 65	66 – 70	71 – 75
Frequency	2	7	17	25	19	8	2

2   26   51   70   78   80

Spread of Data

Averages and "Spread"

1) **AVERAGES** are used to <u>compare</u> sets of data. Take a look at this example:

> **EXAMPLE** Below are the results of Steve's and Sachin's last 10 Physics tests.
> <u>Use these results to say who is better at Physics</u>.
>
> | <u>Steve</u>: Mean mark = 22.6 | <u>Sachin</u>: Mean mark = 34.4 |
> |---|---|
> | Median mark = 24 | Median mark = 33.5 |
> | Modal mark = 16 | Modal mark = 33 |
> | Range = 18 | Range = 8 |
>
> <u>ANS</u>: Sachin's mean, median and modal marks are all higher than Steve's,
> so "<u>the results suggest that Sachin is better at Physics</u>".

2) The **RANGE** is used to compare the **SPREAD** of data. So going back to the example — Steve's range of marks is a lot bigger than Sachin's, which means that his <u>spread of marks is greater</u>. In other words, <u>Sachin's marks are more consistent</u>.

Shapes of Histograms and "Spread"

You can easily estimate the <u>mean</u> from the shape of a histogram — it's more or less <u>in the middle</u>.

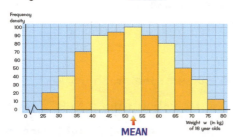

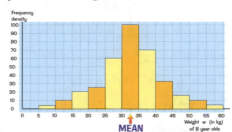

You must <u>LEARN what the shapes</u> of these two histograms tell you about the <u>spread</u> of the data:

1) The first shows <u>high dispersion</u> — a <u>large spread</u> of results away from the mean. So the weights in this sample of 16 year olds are spread out over a wide range.

2) The second shows a "<u>tighter</u>" distribution of results where most values are within a <u>narrow range</u> either side of the mean. So the weights in this sample of 8 year olds show <u>little</u> variation.

Cumulative Freq. Curves and "Spread"

The shape of a **CUMULATIVE FREQUENCY CURVE** also tells us <u>how spread out</u> the data values are.

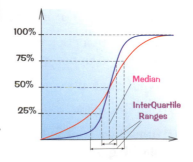

1) The steep blue curve shows a <u>small interquartile range</u> — i.e. a <u>very tight distribution</u> around the **MEDIAN**.

2) The less steep red curve shows a <u>larger interquartile range</u> — i.e. a more <u>widely spread</u> set of data.

Suppose that the two curves shown represent the <u>lifetimes of light bulbs</u> for two different brands. The brand represented by the blue graph is the <u>better product</u> as the lifetimes are <u>more consistent</u>. The lifetimes of the other brand show <u>wide variation</u> which shows that the bulbs are not as reliable.

Revision Summary for Module Eight

Phew, that's another module almost done with. You're on the home straight and going for glory...
Well, perhaps not that exciting, but you see what I'm getting at. Go through these questions and
don't forget to go back and revise anything you don't know. Good luck.

1) What's the format of numbers written in <u>standard form</u>? What <u>three rules</u> should you remember?

2) What four types of <u>percentage problems</u> should you know? Do a simple example for each.

3) What's the method for <u>multiplying out brackets</u> such as $3(2x + 4)$?

4) What does <u>D.O.T.S.</u> stand for? Give two examples of it.

5) What are the <u>six steps</u> for <u>solving equations</u> or <u>rearranging formulas</u>? What's the 7th step?

6) What are the <u>six steps</u> for doing <u>simultaneous equations</u>? How do you solve them with <u>graphs</u>?

7) Write down <u>four important details</u> for <u>factorising quadratics</u>. How do you get the <u>solutions</u>?

8) What is the <u>four-stage method</u> for <u>graphical inequalities</u>?

9) What are the three main types of straight lines you should know?

10) What do all other straight-line equations look like?

11) Describe how you use the "x = 0, y = 0" method to draw a straight line.

12) What kind of equations are written in the form "y = mx + c"? What do "m" and "c" represent?

13) List the <u>five steps</u> needed to draw the graph of $5x = 2 + y$ using <u>y = mx + c</u>.

14) What is the formula for <u>gradient</u>? Write down the four-step method for finding it.

15) How are the gradients of <u>parallel lines</u> related?

16) Sketch the graphs of $y = x^3$ and $y = \frac{1}{x}$. Describe the shape of the graph $y = -x^3$.

17) How do you tackle "what combination of transformations takes you from A to B" questions?

18) Describe <u>enlargements</u> with these <u>scale factors</u>: greater than 1, between 0 and 1, less than 0.

19) What are the three key rules to remember for <u>dimensional analysis</u>?

20) The method for doing <u>trigonometry problems</u> is long, but it always works. Write it out in full.

21) What do the angles of <u>elevation</u> and <u>depression</u> show? How are their values related?

22) Write down the <u>four important facts</u> about <u>tree diagrams</u>.

23) Draw a <u>general tree diagram</u> and put all the features on it.

24) If two events are <u>independent</u>, what can you say about their probabilities?

25) There are four other important things you need to know about probability. What are they?

26) Write down <u>four key points</u> about <u>cumulative frequency</u>.

27) Draw a typical <u>cumulative frequency curve</u>, and mark on the <u>median</u> and lower and upper <u>quartiles</u>. Draw a <u>box plot</u> underneath your curve.

28) What does the <u>range</u> of a set of data tell you about the data?

29) Can you deduce anything about the <u>spread</u> of a set of data from the <u>shape of the histogram</u>?

30) Draw two contrasting cumulative frequency curves — one showing <u>high dispersion</u> and the other showing a <u>tight distribution</u>.

31) Which <u>numerical figure</u> represents spread on a cumulative frequency curve?

Calculation Bounds

You should be confident about rounding numbers to a certain number of <u>decimal places</u> or <u>significant figures</u>. *If not, it's covered on page 1.* Things get trickier when they start asking about the <u>maximum</u> and <u>minimum possible values</u> for a <u>given accuracy</u>...

1) <u>Upper</u> and <u>Lower</u> bounds of a <u>Measurement</u>

The simple rule is this:

> **The real value can be as much as HALF THE ROUNDED UNIT above and below the rounded-off value.**

E.g. If a length is given as 2.4 m to the nearest 0.1 m, the rounded unit is 0.1 m so the real value could be anything up to 2.4 m ± 0.05 m giving answers of 2.45 m and 2.35 m for the upper and lower bounds.

2) <u>Maximum</u> and <u>Minimum</u> Values for Calculations

When a calculation is done using rounded-off values there will be a <u>DISCREPANCY</u> between the <u>CALCULATED VALUE</u> and the <u>ACTUAL VALUE</u>:

<u>EXAMPLE 1</u>: A floor is measured as being 5.3 m × 4.2 m to the nearest 10 cm. This gives an area of <u>22.26 m²</u>, but this is not the actual floor area because

the real values could be anything from <u>5.25 m to 5.35 m</u> and <u>4.15 m to 4.25 m</u>,

∴ Maximum possible floor area = 5.35 × 4.25 = <u>22.7375</u> m²,

∴ Minimum possible floor area = 5.25 × 4.15 = <u>21.7875</u> m².

<u>EXAMPLE 2</u>: A length, m, is given by the formula: $m = \dfrac{A}{h} - n$

A, h and n are measured to 2 d.p. as follows:

A = 50.13 m², h = 12.12 m, n = 3.46 m. Find the max. and min. possible values of m.

First of all, work out the <u>range of possible values</u> for each measurement:

> – <u>A</u> could be anything from <u>50.125 to 50.135</u>.
> – <u>h</u> could be anything from <u>12.115 to 12.125</u>.
> – <u>n</u> could be anything from <u>3.455 to 3.465</u>.

Now you've got to work out which value of A, h and n to use. This is the <u>tricky bit</u>. Look at the <u>formula</u> and think what would happen to m as A, h or n gets bigger. You should be able to see that for a <u>maximum value of m</u>... you need <u>A to be as big as possible</u>, but <u>h and n</u> to be as <u>small as possible</u>. And for the <u>minimum value of m</u>, you obviously need the exact opposite.

So... Maximum possible value of m = 50.135 / 12.115 − 3.455 = **0.683 m** (3 d.p.)

Minimum possible value of m = 50.125 / 12.125 − 3.465 = **0.669 m** (3 d.p.)

The Acid Test:

LEARN all the BITS AND BOBS on this page then TURN OVER and see how much you can remember.

1) x and y are measured as **2.32 m** and **0.45 m** to the nearest **0.01 m**.
   a) Find the upper and lower bounds of x and y.
   b) If z = x + 1/y, find the max and min possible values of z.

Careful here — the biggest input values don't always give the biggest result.

Powers

Powers are a very useful shorthand: $2 \times 2 \times 2 \times 2 \times 2 = 2^5$ ("two to the power 5")

The <u>Seven</u> Easy Rules:

The first two only work for powers of the same number.

1) When <u>MULTIPLYING</u>, you <u>ADD THE POWERS</u>. e.g. $3^4 \times 3^6 = 3^{6+4} = 3^{10}$

2) When <u>DIVIDING</u>, you <u>SUBTRACT THE POWERS</u>. e.g. $5^4 \div 5^2 = 5^{4-2} = 5^2$

3) When <u>RAISING one power to another</u>, you <u>MULTIPLY THEM</u>. e.g. $(3^2)^4 = 3^{2 \times 4} = 3^8$

4) $X^1 = X$, <u>ANYTHING</u> to the <u>POWER 1</u> is just <u>ITSELF</u>. e.g. $3^1 = 3$, $6 \times 6^3 = 6^4$

5) $X^0 = 1$, <u>ANYTHING</u> to the <u>POWER 0</u> is just <u>ONE</u>. e.g. $5^0 = 1$ $67^0 = 1$

6) $1^x = 1$, <u>1 TO ANY POWER</u> is <u>STILL JUST 1</u>. e.g. $1^{23} = 1$ $1^{89} = 1$ $1^2 = 1$

7) <u>FRACTIONS</u> — Apply power to <u>both TOP and BOTTOM</u>. e.g. $\left(1\tfrac{3}{5}\right)^3 = \left(\dfrac{8}{5}\right)^3 = \dfrac{8^3}{5^3} = \dfrac{512}{125}$

The <u>Two</u> Tricky Rules:

8) NEGATIVE POWERS — TURN IT UPSIDE-DOWN

People do have quite a bit of difficulty remembering this.
Whenever you see a negative power you're supposed to immediately think:
"Aha, that means turn it the other way up and make the power positive"
Like this: **e.g.** $7^{-2} = \dfrac{1}{7^2} = \dfrac{1}{49}$ $\left(\dfrac{3}{5}\right)^{-2} = \left(\dfrac{5}{3}\right)^{+2} = \dfrac{5^2}{3^2} = \dfrac{25}{9}$

9) FRACTIONAL POWERS

> The Power ½ means <u>Square Root</u>,
> The Power ⅓ means <u>Cube Root</u>,
> The Power ¼ means <u>Fourth Root</u> etc.

e.g. $25^{\frac{1}{2}} = \sqrt{25} = 5$
$64^{\frac{1}{3}} = \sqrt[3]{64} = 4$
$81^{\frac{1}{4}} = \sqrt[4]{81} = 3$ etc.

The one to really watch is when you get a <u>negative fraction</u> like $49^{-\frac{1}{2}}$ — people get mixed up and think that the minus is the square root, and forget to turn it upside down as well.

Example: "Evaluate a) 8^0 b) 2^{-3} c) $8^{\frac{2}{3}}$"

using rule 3 backwards

ANSWER: a) $8^0 = 1$ b) $2^{-3} = \dfrac{1}{2^3} = \dfrac{1}{8}$ c) $8^{\frac{2}{3}} = 8^{\frac{1}{3} \times 2} = (8^{\frac{1}{3}})^2 = 2^2 = 4$

using rule 5   rule 8 — turn it upside down   split it into a root and a power and do the <u>root first</u>

Example: "Simplify without a calculator, giving your answer in standard form: $\dfrac{4 \times 10^4}{5 \times 10^{-6}}$"

For standard form, see p54 of module 8.

ANSWER: $\dfrac{4 \times 10^4}{5 \times 10^{-6}} = \dfrac{4}{5} \times \dfrac{10^4}{10^{-6}} = 0.8 \times 10^4 \div 10^{-6} = 0.8 \times 10^{10} = 8 \times 10^9$

First, separate out the number bits from the "$\times 10$" bits.   Now using rule 2, subtract the powers.   Finally, put it into standard form — the number has to be between 1 and 10, remember.

The Acid Test:

LEARN ALL NINE Exciting Rules on this page. Then **TURN OVER** and write them all down with examples. Keep trying till you can.

1) Simplify: a) $4^3 \times 4^5$ b) $3^6 / 3^3$ c) $(2^3)^4$ d) $(2^3 \times 2^5 \times 2^6)/2^8$ e) $6^2 \times 6 \times 6^3$

2) Evaluate a) $(\tfrac{1}{4})^{-3}$ b) 25^{-2} c) $25^{-\frac{1}{2}}$ d) $\left(\tfrac{27}{216}\right)^{-\frac{1}{3}}$ e) $625^{\frac{3}{4}}$ f) $125^{-\frac{2}{3}}$

3) Use your calculator to find: a) 5.2^{24} b) $40^{\frac{3}{4}}$ c) $\sqrt[5]{200}$

Basic Algebra

Before embarking on the epic journey downwards to the bottom of this page, have a look at p57 of module 8 on multiplying out brackets and D.O.T.S. — you need them for module 9 too.

Factorising — Putting Brackets In

Factorising quadratics into two brackets is a special case and is covered separately on pages 62 and 82.

Factorising just involves taking common factors outside a bracket:

1) Take out the biggest number that goes into all the terms.
2) Take each letter in turn and take out the highest power (e.g. x, x^2 etc) that will go into EVERY term.
3) Open the brackets and fill in all the bits needed to reproduce each term.

EXAMPLE: "Factorise $15x^4y + 20x^2y^3z - 35x^3yz^2$"

ANSWER: $5x^2y(3x^2 + 4y^2z - 7xz^2)$

Biggest number that'll divide into 15, 20 and 35.

Highest powers of x and y that will go into all three terms.

z was not in ALL terms so it can't come out as a common factor.

REMEMBER:
1) The bits taken out and put at the front are the common factors.
2) The bits inside the brackets are what's needed to get back to the original terms if you multiply the brackets out again.

Cancelling Down Algebraic Fractions

This is fairly painless — anything being multiplied on the top and bottom of a fraction can be cancelled. What you're actually doing is dividing the top and bottom by that thing. You have to be a bit careful when things are raised to powers though...

E.g. $$\frac{x^4(x-1)(x+2)}{(x+2)(x-1)^2x^2} = \frac{x^4(x-1)(x+2)}{(x+2)(x-1)^2x^2} = \frac{x^4(x-1)}{(x-1)^2x^2} = \frac{x^4}{(x-1)x^2} = \frac{x^2}{(x-1)}$$

There's an (x+2) on the top and bottom to be cancelled.

Remember that $(x-1)^2$ is just $(x-1)(x-1)$, so cancelling $(x-1)$ leaves an $(x-1)$ on the bottom.

Now there's an x^2 on the top ($x^4 = x^2 \times x^2$) and bottom. Cancelling leaves x^2 on the top.

Exam questions try to make things harder by expecting you to factorise at the start:

EXAMPLE: Simplify $\frac{x^2-9}{x^2-4x-21}$

The top will factorise using D.O.T.S. (see p57)

The bottom expression is a typical quadratic expression, so see if it'll factorise (see p62 or p82) — I have a feeling it will...

ANSWER: $\frac{x^2-9}{x^2-4x-21} = \frac{(x+3)(x-3)}{(x+3)(x-7)} = \frac{(x-3)}{(x-7)}$

The Acid Test:
Learn the methods for factorising and cancelling algebraic fractions, then try the questions below.

1) Factorise $12x^2yz + 4xy^2z$

2) Simplify $\frac{x^2+2x-15}{x^2-25}$

Direct and Inverse Proportion

Direct Proportion: y = kx
BOTH INCREASE TOGETHER

Inverse Proportion: y = k/x
One **INCREASES** , one **DECREASES**

1) The graph of y against x is a <u>straight line through the origin: y = kx</u>

The graph of y against x is the well known y = k/x graph:

2) In a table of values the **MULTIPLIER** is the <u>same for x and y</u>, i.e. if you <u>double</u> one of them, you <u>double</u> the other; if you <u>times one of them by 3</u>, you <u>times the other by 3</u>, etc.

In a table of values the **MULTIPLIER** for one of them becomes a **DIVIDER** for the other, i.e. if you <u>double one</u>, you <u>half the other</u>, if you <u>treble one</u>, you <u>divide the other by three</u>, etc.

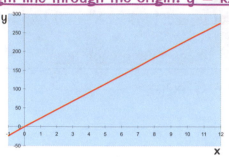

x	2	6	8	12	14	56
y	3	9	12	18	21	84

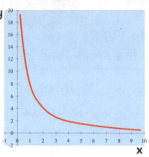

x	2	6	8	12	40	10
y	30	10	7.5	5	1.5	6

3) The <u>**RATIO**</u> x/y <u>is the same</u> <u>for all pairs</u> of values, i.e from the table above:

$$\frac{2}{3} = \frac{6}{9} = \frac{8}{12} = \frac{12}{18} = \frac{14}{21} = \frac{56}{84} = 0.6667$$

The <u>**PRODUCT**</u> xy (x times y) is the <u>same</u> for <u>all pairs of values</u>, i.e. in the table above:

$$2 \times 30 = 6 \times 10 = 8 \times 7.5 = 12 \times 5$$
$$= 40 \times 1.5 = 10 \times 6 = \underline{60}$$

Inverse Square Variation

You can have all sorts of relationships between x and y, like $y = kx^2$ or $y = k/x^3$ etc. as detailed on the next page. The most important type is <u>$y = k/x^2$</u> and is called "<u>**INVERSE SQUARE**</u>" variation.

<u>**DON'T MIX UP THIS NAME**</u> with <u>inverse proportion</u>, which is just $y = k/x$.

The Acid Test:
LEARN the 3 KEY FEATURES for both <u>Direct</u> and <u>Inverse</u> proportion. Then <u>turn over</u> and <u>write them all down</u>.

1) Give examples of 2 real quantities that exhibit a) direct- and b) inverse proportion.
2) Make up your own tables of values which show
     a) DIRECT PROPORTION   b) INVERSE PROPORTION

Direct and Inverse Proportion

This page shows you how to deal with questions which involve statements like these:
"y is proportional to the square of x"   "t is proportional to the square root of h"
"D varies with the cube of t"   "V is inversely proportional to r cubed"

To deal successfully with things like this <u>you must remember this method</u>:

Method:

1) <u>Convert the sentence into a proportionality</u>

   using the symbol " $\propto$ " which means "<u>is proportional to</u>"

2) <u>Replace " $\propto$ " with "=k"</u> to make an **EQUATION**:

The above examples would become:	Proportionality	Equation
"y is proportional to the square of x"	$y \propto x^2$	$y = kx^2$
"t is proportional to the square root of h"	$t \propto \sqrt{h}$	$t = k\sqrt{h}$
"D varies with the cube of t"	$D \propto t^3$	$D = kt^3$
"V is inversely proportional to r cubed"	$V \propto 1/r^3$	$V = k/r^3$

   (Once you've got it in the form of an equation with k, <u>the rest is easy</u>.)

3) <u>Find a **PAIR OF VALUES** of x and y</u> somewhere in the question, and
   <u>**SUBSTITUTE** them into the equation</u> with the <u>sole purpose of finding k</u>.

4) <u>Put the value of k back into the equation</u>
   and it's now ready to use, e.g. $y = 3x^2$

5) <u>**INEVITABLY**, they'll ask you to find y</u>,
   having given you a value for x (or vice versa).

Example:

The time taken for a duck to fall down a chimney (it happens!) is inversely proportional
to the square of the diameter of the flue. If she took 25 seconds to descend a chimney
of diameter 0.3m, how long would it take her to get down one of 0.2m diameter?

(Notice there's no mention of "writing an equation" or "finding k" — it's up to **YOU** to remember
the method for yourself.)

ANSWER:
1) Write it as a <u>proportionality</u>, then an <u>equation</u>: $t \propto 1/d^2$ i.e. $t = k/d^2$
2) <u>Sub in the given values</u> for the two variables: $25 = k/0.3^2$
3) Rearrange the equation to <u>find k</u>: $k = 25 \times 0.3^2 = 2.25$
4) Put k <u>back in</u> the formula: $t = 2.25/d^2$
5) <u>Sub in new value</u> for d: $t = 2.25/0.2^2 = \underline{56.25 \text{ s}}$

The Acid Test:
LEARN the **FIVE STEPS** of the **METHOD** plus the <u>four
examples</u>. Then <u>turn over and write them all down</u>.

1) The frequency of a pendulum is inversely proportional to the square root of its length. If the
pendulum swings with a frequency of 0.5 Hz when the length is 80 cm, what frequency will it have
with a length of 50 cm, and what length will give a frequency of 0.7 Hz?

Quadratic Equations

Before you even look at this page, have a good read through p62 from module 8 which shows you how to factorise and solve a quadratic equation $ax^2 + bx + c = 0$ when $a = 1$. OK good. Now when a is not 1, the basic method is still the same, it's just a lot messier...

Solving $ax^2 + bx + c = 0$ when "a" is not 1

EXAMPLE: "Solve $3x^2 + 7x + 2 = 8$ by factorising."

1) **First rearrange it** (into the standard format): $3x^2 + 7x - 6 = 0$

2) Now because $a = 3$, the two x-terms in the brackets will have to multiply to give $3x^2$ so the initial brackets will have to be: $(3x\quad)(x\quad)=0$

   (i.e. you put in the x-terms first, with coefficients that will multiply to give "a")

3) We now want to look at all pairs of numbers that multiply with each other to give "c" (=6, ignoring the minus sign for now): i.e. 1×6 and 2×3

4) **Now the difficult bit**: to find the combination which does this:

   > multiply with the 3x and x terms in the brackets and then add or subtract to give the value of b (=7):

   The best way to do this is by trying out all the possibilities in the brackets until you find the combination that works. Don't forget that **EACH PAIR** of numbers can be tried in **TWO** different positions:

   $(3x\quad 1)(x\quad 6)$ multiplies to give 18x and 1x which add/subtract to give 17x or 19x
   $(3x\quad 6)(x\quad 1)$ multiplies to give 3x and 6x which add/subtract to give 9x or 3x
   $(3x\quad 3)(x\quad 2)$ multiplies to give 6x and 3x which add/subtract to give 9x or 3x
   $(3x\quad 2)(x\quad 3)$ multiplies to give 9x and 2x which add/subtract to give 11x or ⑦x

   So $(3x\quad 2)(x\quad 3)$ is the combination that gives b = 7, (give or take a +/–)

5) **Now fill in the +/– signs** so that the combination will add/subtract to give +7 (=b). Clearly it must be -2 and +3 which give rise to -2x and +9x. So the final brackets are: $(3x - 2)(x + 3)$

6) **As an ESSENTIAL check, EXPAND the brackets** out again to make sure they give the original equation:
   $(3x - 2)(x + 3) = 3x^2 + 9x - 2x - 6 = 3x^2 + 7x - 6$

7) The last step is to get **THE SOLUTIONS TO THE EQUATION**: $(3x - 2)(x + 3) = 0$ which you do by separately putting each bracket = 0 :

   i.e. $(3x - 2) = 0 \Rightarrow x = 2/3$ $(x + 3) = 0 \Rightarrow x = -3$

   Don't forget that last step. Remember, it's the difference between **SOLVING THE EQUATION** and merely factorising it.

The Acid Test:
LEARN the 7 steps for solving quadratics by factorising when "a ≠ 1".

1) Solve by factorising: a) $5x^2 - 17x - 12 = 0$ b) $6x^2 + 7x - 3 = 0$ c) $8x^2 - 13x + 5 = 0$

Straight Lines

Before you get started, have a look back at pages 64-66 from Module 8 on straight-lines.
On page 65 you saw how to draw straight lines from equations, now you've got the <u>reverse</u>
<u>process</u> — you have to <u>find the equation</u> from the graph.

Finding the Equation Of a Straight Line Graph

METHOD:

1) From the axes, <u>identify the two variables</u>
   (e.g. "x and y" or "h and t").
2) <u>Find the values</u> of "<u>m</u>" (gradient)
   and "<u>c</u>" (y-intercept) from the graph.
3) Using these values from the graph,
   <u>write down the equation</u> with the
   standard format "y = mx + c".

Pick two points on the line and complete
the triangle. For variables X and Y:
GRADIENT = CHANGE IN Y / CHANGE IN X
(see page 66 for more on this).

EXAMPLE:
'Find the equation of the straight line shown.'

ANSWER:

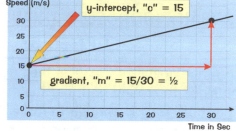

1) The axes are 'Speed' and 'Time' so call
   the variables <u>s and t</u>.

2) To find the <u>gradient</u> (m) choose two points,
   say (0, 15) and (30, 30). Gradient is then (30 – 15) ÷ (30 – 0) = 15 ÷ 30 = <u>½</u>.
   The line hits the y-axis at (0, 15), so the <u>y-intercept</u> (c) is <u>15</u>.

3) Put m = ½ and c = 15 into the equation <u>s = mt + c</u> to get <u>s = ½t + 15</u>.

Parallel and Perpendicular Lines

1) The equation of a straight line is <u>y = mx + c</u>,
   where <u>m</u> is the <u>gradient</u> and c is the y-intercept.

2) Parallel lines have the <u>same value of m</u>, i.e. the <u>same gradient</u>.
   So the lines: y = 2x + 3, y = 2x and y = 2x – 4 are all parallel.

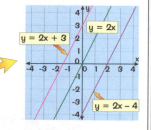

3) The gradients of two <u>perpendicular</u> lines multiply to give <u>–1</u>.

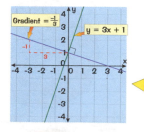

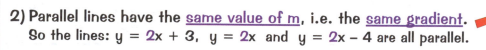

If the gradient of the first line is m, the gradient of
the other line will be $\frac{-1}{m}$, because $m \times \frac{-1}{m} = -1$.

The Acid Test:
LEARN the 3 steps for finding the equation of a straight line, and
the <u>rules for parallel and perpendicular lines</u>. Then <u>write</u> it all down.

1) Find the equation of the straight line passing through the points (0, 2) and (8, 18).
2) Find the equation of the line perpendicular to this line, which cuts the y-axis at (0, 4).

Circle Geometry

9 Simple Rules — That's all:

1) ANGLE IN A SEMICIRCLE = 90°

A triangle drawn from the two ends of a diameter will ALWAYS make an angle of 90° where it hits the edge of the circle, no matter where it hits.

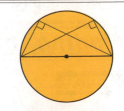

2) TANGENT-RADIUS MEET AT 90°

A TANGENT is a line that just touches a single point on the edge of the circle. A tangent always makes an angle of exactly 90° with the radius it meets at this point.

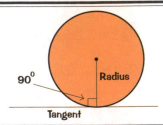

3) SNEAKY ISOSCELES TRIANGLES FORMED BY TWO RADII

Unlike other isosceles triangles they don't have the little tick marks on the sides to remind you that they are the same — the fact that they are both radii is enough to make it an isosceles triangle.

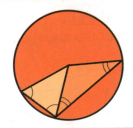

4) CHORD BISECTOR IS A DIAMETER

A CHORD is any line drawn across a circle. And no matter where you draw a chord, the line that cuts it exactly in half (at 90°), will go through the centre of the circle and so will be a DIAMETER.

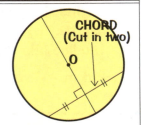

5) ANGLES IN THE SAME SEGMENT ARE EQUAL

All triangles drawn from a chord will have the same angle where they touch the circle. Also, the two angles on opposite sides of the chord add up to 180°.

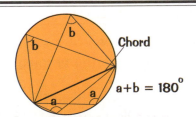

6) ANGLE AT THE CENTRE IS TWICE THE ANGLE AT THE EDGE

The angle subtended at the centre of a circle is EXACTLY DOUBLE the angle subtended at the edge of the circle from the same two points (two ends of the same chord). The phrase "angle subtended at" is nothing complicated, it's just a bit posher than saying "angle made at".

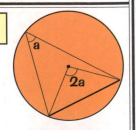

7) OPPOSITE ANGLES OF A CYCLIC QUADRILATERAL ADD UP TO 180°

$a+c=180°$
$b+d=180°$

A cyclic quadrilateral is a 4-sided shape with every corner touching the circle. Both pairs of opposite angles add up to 180°.

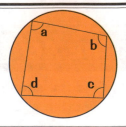

Circle Geometry

8) EQUALITY OF TANGENTS FROM A POINT

The two tangents drawn from an outside point are <u>always equal in length</u>, so creating an "isosceles" situation, with <u>two congruent right-angled triangles</u>.

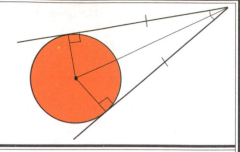

9) ANGLE IN OPPOSITE SEGMENT IS EQUAL

This is perhaps the trickiest one to remember. If you draw a <u>tangent</u> and a <u>chord</u> that meet, then <u>the angle between them</u> is always <u>equal</u> to *"the angle in the opposite segment"* (i.e. the angle made at the edge of the circle by two lines drawn from the chord).

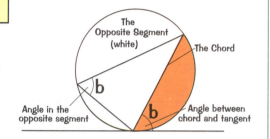

3-Letter Notation for Angles

1) <u>Angles are specified using 3 letters</u>, e.g. angle ODC = 48⁰
2) <u>THE MIDDLE LETTER IS WHERE THE ANGLE IS</u>
3) <u>THE OTHER TWO LETTERS</u> tell you <u>which lines enclose the angle</u>
   For example: Angle ODC is <u>at D</u> and
<u>enclosed by the lines</u> going from <u>O to D</u> and from <u>D to C</u>.

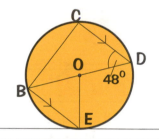

Example

"<u>Find all the angles in this diagram</u>."

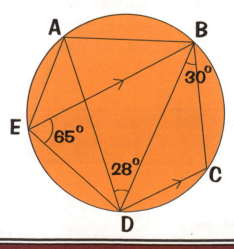

1) <u>PARALLEL LINES</u> — there are actually <u>4 different lines</u> crossing the 2 parallel ones, but the most useful one is ED which tells us that <u>EDC is 115⁰</u>

2) <u>ANGLE IN SAME SEGMENT</u> — there are potentially <u>eight different chords</u> where this rule could apply, but some are more useful than others:
   EAD = EBD,   ADB = AEB (so AEB = <u>28°</u>)
   ABE = ADE,   DAB = DEB (so DAB = <u>65°</u>)

3) <u>OPPOSITE ANGLES OF A CYCLIC QUADRILATERAL</u>
   — looking at BEDC gives:
   BCD = 180 – DEB = 180 – 65 = <u>115°</u>
   — looking at ABDE gives:
   ABD = 180 – AED = 180 – (28 + 65) = <u>87°</u>

4) <u>ANGLES IN A TRIANGLE ADD UP TO 180°</u> — this, the simplest of all the rules, will now find all the other angles for you.

The Acid Test:

LEARN all <u>Nine Rules</u> on these two pages. Then <u>turn over and write them all down</u>.

1) Find all the angles in the 3rd diagram above illustrating the 3-letter notation (ODC = 48°, etc.).
2) <u>Practise the above example</u> till you <u>understand every step</u> and can do it easily without help.

Length, Area and Volume

Now for some of the lesser used (but not lesser-tested-in-the-exam) formulas. Eek.

Arcs & Sectors

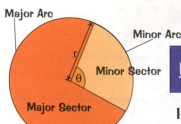

Major Arc
Minor Arc
Minor Sector
Major Sector

$$\text{Area of Sector} = \frac{\theta}{360} \times \text{Area of full Circle}$$

(Pretty obvious really isn't it?)

$$\text{Length of Arc} = \frac{\theta}{360} \times \text{Circumference of full Circle}$$

(Obvious again, no?)

If you need a swift reminder, the Area of a Circle = πr^2
and Circumference = $\pi d = 2\pi r$

Spheres

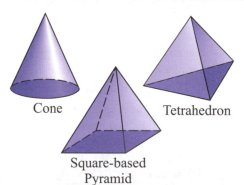

$$\text{Volume of sphere} = \frac{4}{3}\pi r^3$$

EXAMPLE: The moon has a radius of 1700km, find its volume.

Ans: $V = \frac{4}{3}\pi r^3 = (4/3) \times 3.14 \times 1700^3 = 2.1 \times 10^{10}$ km³   (A lot of cheese)

Pyramids and Cones

A pyramid is any shape that goes up to a point at the top. Its base can be any shape at all.
If the base is a circle then it's called a cone (rather than a circular pyramid).

Cone

Tetrahedron

Square-based Pyramid

$$\text{Volume of Pyramid} = \frac{1}{3} \times \text{Base Area} \times \text{Height}$$

$$\text{Volume of Cone} = \frac{1}{3} \times \pi r^2 \times \text{Height}$$

This surprisingly simple formula is true for any pyramid or cone, whether it goes up "vertically" (like the three shown here) or off to one side (like the one at the bottom of the page).

The Acid Test:

LEARN this page. Then turn over and try to write it all down. Keep trying until you can do it.

1) Name the shape below and find its volume.

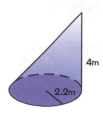

4m

2.2m

2) Find the perimeter and area of this shape.
You'll need to make use of Pythagoras and/or trigonometry to solve this one.
(See p43, 70 and 71.)

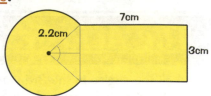

2.2cm

7cm

3cm

Enlargements and Line Segments

On this page we will tackle <u>enlargements</u> and <u>line segments</u> — two topics which frankly go together about as well <u>penguins</u> and <u>paragliding</u>. Ho hum, here they are anyway...

Areas and Volumes of Enlargements

Ho ho! This little joker catches everybody out. The increase in area and volume is <u>BIGGER</u> than the scale factor.

<u>For example</u>, if the <u>Scale Factor is 2</u>, the lengths are <u>twice as big</u>, each area is <u>4 times</u> as big, and the volume is <u>8 times</u> as big. The rule is this:

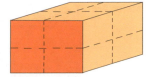

<u>For a Scale Factor n</u>:

The <u>SIDES</u> are   n times bigger

The <u>AREAS</u> are n^2 times bigger

The <u>VOLUMES</u> are n^3 times bigger

Simple... but <u>VERY FORGETTABLE</u>

These ratios can also be expressed in this form:

Lengths	$a : b$	e.g. $3 : 4$
Areas	$a^2 : b^2$	e.g. $9 : 16$
Volumes	$a^3 : b^3$	e.g. $27 : 64$

<u>EXAMPLE</u>:

2 spheres have surface areas of $16m^2$ and $25m^2$. Find the ratio of their volumes.

<u>ANS</u>: $16 : 25$ is the areas ratio which must be $a^2 : b^2$,

i.e. $a^2 : b^2 = 16 : 25$

and so $a : b = 4 : 5$

and so $a^3 : b^3 = \underline{64 : 125}$ — the volumes ratio.

Line Segments — an excuse for more Pythagoras

Don't panic. You've <u>done this all before</u>. This is another sneaky way that examiners use to test your <u>Pythagoras</u> (p43) and <u>coordinates</u> (p45) knowledge at the <u>same time</u>.

Make sure you have a <u>labelled diagram</u> (sketch one if they don't give you one).

<u>EXAMPLE</u>:   *"Find the length of the line segment shown."*

❶   Work out <u>how far across and up</u> it is from <u>A to B</u>
❷   Treat this exactly like a <u>normal triangle</u>...
❸   <u>Square them</u>*: $3^2 = 9$, $4^2 = 16$
❹   You want to find the <u>longest side</u> (the hypotenuse),
              so <u>ADD</u>: $9 + 16 = 25$
❺   <u>Square root</u>: $\sqrt{25} = 5$
          So the <u>length of the line segment = 5 units</u>

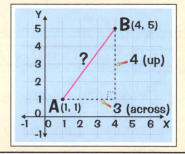

* Pythagoras' Theorem is $a^2 + b^2 = c^2$ if you need a reminder.

The Acid Test:

<u>LEARN</u> the <u>Rules for Area and Volume Ratios</u>. Then get your head around <u>line segments</u>. Then <u>turn over and write it all down</u>.

1) Two monkeys are mathematically similar. One is 30cm tall and the surface area of his skin is 1100 cm^2. The skin of the other is 2200cm^2, how tall is he?

2) Two similar cones have volumes of $27m^3$ and $64m^3$. If the surface area of the smaller one is $36m^2$, find the surface area of the other one.

3) Find the length of a line segment which runs between A(1,5) and B(5,1).

3D Pythagoras and Trigonometry

3D questions on Pythagoras and trig might seem a bit mind-boggling at first
— but you're really just using those same old rules.

Angle Between Line and Plane — Use a Diagram

Learn The 3-Step Method

1) Make a RIGHT-ANGLED triangle using the line, a line in the plane and a line between the two.

2) Draw this right-angled triangle again so that you can see it clearly. Label the sides. You might have to use Pythagoras to work out the length of one of the sides.

3) Use trigonometry to calculate the angle.

Example: "ABCDE is a square-based pyramid. It is 12 cm high and the square base has sides of length 7 cm. Find the angle the edge AE makes with the base."

X is the centre of the square base.

1) First draw a right-angled triangle using the edge AE, the base and a line between the two (in this case the central height). Call the angle you're trying to find θ.

2) Now draw this triangle clearly and label it.

To find θ, you need to know the length of side EX.

So, using Pythagoras — $EX^2 = 3.5^2 + 3.5^2 = 24.5 \Rightarrow EX = \sqrt{24.5}$ cm

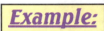 You know the lengths of the **opposite** and **adjacent** sides, so use **tan**.

3) Now use trigonometry to find the angle θ:

$$\tan \theta = \frac{12}{\sqrt{24.5}} = 2.4... \quad \theta = \underline{67.6°} \text{ (1 d.p.)}$$

Use Right-Angled Triangles To Find Lengths too

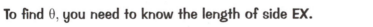

Example: "Find the lengths FH and BH shown in the diagram."

1) First use Pythagoras to find the length FH.

$FH^2 = 3^2 + 3^2 = 18 \Rightarrow FH = \sqrt{18}$ cm

2) Now use Pythagoras again to find the length BH.

$BH^2 = 3^2 + (\sqrt{18})^2 = 27 \Rightarrow BH = \sqrt{27}$ cm $= \underline{5.2 \text{ cm}}$ (1 decimal place)

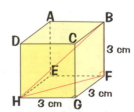

The Acid Test:

LEARN THE 3-STEP METHOD — then try the questions below.

1) Calculate the angle that the line AG makes with the base of this cuboid.

2) Calculate the length of AG.

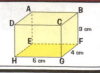

Probability

You might feel the need to ease gently into probability by having a quick look over the basics. If so, have a look back at pages 21-22 in Module 6, and pages 72-73 in Module 8. This page gives you the method for solving more complicated probability problems.

The Steps

1) **Always break down** a complicated-looking probability question into **A SEQUENCE** of **SEPARATE SINGLE EVENTS**.
2) **Find the probability of EACH** of these **SEPARATE SINGLE EVENTS**.
3) **Apply the AND/OR rule:**

The Rules:

1) The AND Rule:

$$P(A \text{ and } B) = P(A) \times P(B)$$

Which means:

The probability of Event A AND Event B BOTH happening is equal to the two separate probabilities MULTIPLIED together.

(Strictly speaking, the two events have to be INDEPENDENT. All that means is that one event happening does not in any way affect the other one happening. Contrast this with mutually exclusive below.)

2) The OR Rule:

$$P(A \text{ or } B) = P(A) + P(B)$$

Which means:

The probability of EITHER Event A OR Event B happening is equal to the two separate probabilities ADDED together.

(Strictly speaking, the two events have to be MUTUALLY EXCLUSIVE which means that if one event happens, the other one can't happen.)

The way to remember this is that it's the wrong way round — i.e. you'd want the AND to go with the + but it doesn't: It's "AND with ×" and "OR with +".

Example

"Find the probability of picking two kings from a pack of cards (assuming you don't replace the first card picked)."

ANSWER:
1) SPLIT this into TWO SEPARATE EVENTS
— i.e. picking the first king and then picking the second king.

2) Find the SEPARATE probabilities of these two separate events:

$P(\text{1st king}) = \frac{4}{52}$ $P(\text{2nd king}) = \frac{3}{51}$ ← Note the change from 52 to 51 because the first card isn't replaced.

3) Apply the AND/OR rule: BOTH events must happen, so it's the AND rule:

so multiply the two separate probabilities: $\frac{4}{52} \times \frac{3}{51} = \frac{1}{221}$

The Acid Test:
LEARN the Three Simple Steps for multiple events, and the AND/OR Rules.

1) Find the probability of picking from a pack of cards (without replacement):
a) 2 queens plus the ace of spades. b) A pair of Jacks, Queens or Kings.

Histograms

A histogram is just a bar chart where the bars can be of DIFFERENT widths, and the vertical axis shows FREQUENCY DENSITY instead of frequency. This changes them from nice, simple diagrams into seemingly incomprehensible monsters. Well OK, things aren't really that bad, but only if you LEARN THE TWO METHODS for finding the frequencies:

1) Using Areas

It's not the height, but the AREA of each bar that gives the frequency.

> METHOD : 1) Use the snip of information they give you to find HOW MUCH IS REPRESENTED BY EACH AREA BLOCK.
>
> 2) Divide all the bars into THE SAME SIZED AREA BLOCKS and so work out the number for each bar (using AREAS).

EXAMPLE: The histogram below represents the age distribution of people arrested for slurping boiled sweets in public places in 1995. Given that there were 36 people in the 55 to 65 age range, find the number of people arrested in all the other age ranges.

This is the snip of information.

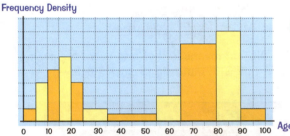

ANSWER: 1) The 55-65 bar represents 36 people and contains 4 dotted squares, so each dotted square must represent 9 people.

2) The rest is easy. E.g. the 80-90 group has 14 dotted squares so that represents $14 \times 9 = $ 126 people.

2) Using the Formula

And that formula is...

> FREQUENCY DENSITY = FREQUENCY ÷ CLASS WIDTH

You need to use this formula if they give you the frequency density values on the y-axis, rather than information about one of the groups.

EXAMPLE CONTINUED:

You need to rearrange the formula.

So for the 80-90 group,
Frequency = Frequency Density × Class Width
$= 12.6 \times 10$
$= $ 126 people (as before)

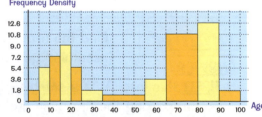

A Couple of Extra Things...

1) You might be given a frequency table and asked to draw a histogram. Just use the formula to find the frequency density values, and plot them on the y-axis.

2) Have a look at p75 in Module 8 to see what the shape of a histogram tells you.

The Acid Test: LEARN this page, then turn over and write down everything you know about histograms.

1) Find the number of people in each of the age ranges for the histogram above.

Sampling methods

This is all about doing surveys of 'populations' (not necessarily people) to find things out about them. Things start getting awkward when you can't test the whole 'population', usually because there's just too many. In that case you have to take a sample, which means you somehow have to select a limited number of individuals so that they properly represent the whole 'population'.

There are TWO DIFFERENT TYPES OF SAMPLING which you should know about:

RANDOM — this is where you just select individuals "at random". In practice it can be surprisingly difficult to make the selection truly random.

STRATIFIED — the population is divided into groups (or "strata"). The sample is then chosen by picking randomly from each of the different groups. This should mean that the sample reflects the whole population. E.g. to survey pupils in a school you would first pick a selection of the classes, and then pick students at random from those classes.

Spotting Problems With Sampling Methods

In practice, the most important thing you should be able to do is spot problems with sampling techniques, which means look for ways that the sample might not be a true reflection of the population. One mildly amusing way to practise is to think up examples of bad sampling techniques:

1) A survey of motorists carried out in London concluded that 85% of British people drive Black Cabs.

2) Two surveys carried out on the same street corner asked, "Do you believe in God?" One found 90% of people didn't and the other found 90% of people did. The reason for the discrepancy? — one was carried out at 11pm Saturday night and the other at 10.15am Sunday morning.

3) A telephone survey carried out in the evening asked, "What do you usually do after work or school?". It found that 80% of the population usually stay in and watch TV. A street survey conducted at the same time found that only 30% usually stay in and watch TV. Astonishing.

Other cases are less obvious...

EXAMPLE:
In a telephone poll, 100 people were asked if they use the train regularly and 20% said yes. Does this mean 20% of the population regularly use the train?

ANSWER: Probably not. There are several things wrong with this sampling technique:

1) First and worst: the sample is far too small. At least 1000 would be more like it.
2) What about people who don't have their own phone?
3) What time of day was it done? When might regular train users be in or out?
4) Which part or parts of the country were telephoned?
5) If the results were to represent say the whole country then stratified sampling would be essential (i.e. you'd need to sample people from every region).

The Acid Test: LEARN the names of the two sampling techniques together with their brief descriptions, and also the 5 points above.

1) A survey was done to investigate the average age of cars on Britain's roads by standing on a motorway bridge and noting the registration of the first 200 cars. Give three reasons why this is a poor sampling technique and suggest a better approach.

Revision Summary for Module Nine

Hurray! You've reached the end of the section — well, almost. But you've still got to read over the following pages from the previous modules. You need to know these topics for module 9 too, so read them properly and make sure you can do them:

– rearranging formulas (p59 module 8)   – estimating and checking (p29 module 7)

– multiplying out brackets and D.O.T.S. (p57 module 8)

OK, now below are twenty or so questions which will show you how much you've actually learned. When you get stuck, look back at the page and go back over that bit. Don't just sit there, get stuck in!

1) What's the simple rule for finding the upper and lower bounds of a measurement?

2) Describe how you'd use these values to find the max and min possible values of a calculation.

3) What are the "seven easy" rules and the "two tricky rules" for dealing with powers?

4) What are the steps for factorising expressions such as $12x^2y^3z + 15x^3yz^2$?

5) What's the "fairly painless" rule for cancelling algebraic fractions?
    Do an example to show it.

6) List the three key features of both direct and inverse proportion.

7) What sort of statements are involved in the subject of variation?

8) List the basic steps for factorising a quadratic when a is not 1.

9) List the three steps for finding the equation of a straight-line graph.

10) How are the gradients of perpendicular lines related?

11) Write down the 9 simple rules for circle geometry.

12) What is three-letter notation? Give an example.

13) Write down the formulas for: a) volume of a pyramid   b) volume of a cone
    c) Volume of a sphere   d) area of a sector   e) length of an arc

14) If length is enlarged by a scale factor of n, how much do area and volume increase by?

15) What two topics are needed for most questions on line segments? Write down the important formula you are likely to need to answer one of these questions.

16) Draw a diagram to illustrate an example where you might have to find the angle between a line and a plane. State the three stage method which should be used on these problems.

17) What are the AND and OR rules of probability?

18) Describe two differences between a histogram and a bar chart.

19) Write down the two-step method for finding histogram frequencies using areas.

20) Write down the formula for frequency density.

21) What is sampling all about? When is it needed?

22) Name the two main sampling methods, and give a brief description of each.

Compound Growth and Decay

This can also be called "Exponential" Growth or Decay.

The Formula

This topic is simple if you **LEARN THIS FORMULA**. If you don't, it's pretty well impossible:

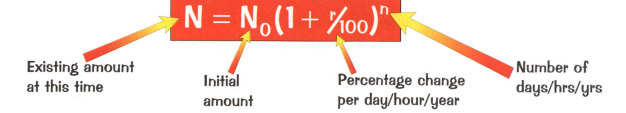

$$N = N_0\left(1 + \tfrac{r}{100}\right)^n$$

Existing amount at this time

Initial amount

Percentage change per day/hour/year

Number of days/hrs/yrs

Percentage Increase and Decrease

The (1 + r/100) bit might look a bit confusing in the formula but in practice it's really easy:

E.g   5% increase will be 1.05   5% decrease will be 0.95   (= 1 – 0.05)
26% increase will be 1.26   26% decrease will be 0.74   (= 1 – 0.26)

3 Examples to show you how EASY it is:

1) "A man invests £1000 in a savings account which pays 8% per annum. How much will there be after 6 years?"

ANSWER: Usual formula: Amount = $1000(1.08)^6$ = **£1586.87**

Initial amount   8% increase   6 years

2) "The activity of a radio-isotope falls by 12% every hour. If the initial activity is 800 counts per minute, what will it be after 7 hours?"

ANSWER: Same old formula:

Activity = Initial value$(1 – 12/100)^n$

Activity = $800(1 – 0.12)^7$ = $800 \times (0.88)^7$ = **327 cpm**

3) "In a sample of bacteria, there are initially 500 cells and they increase in number by 15% each day. Find the formula relating the number of cells, n, and the number of days, d."

ANSWER: Well stone me, it's the same old easy-peasy compound growth formula _again_: $n = n_0(1 + 0.15)^d$ or finished off: **$n = 500 \times (1.15)^d$**

The Acid Test:

LEARN THE FORMULA. Also learn the _3 Examples_. Then _turn over and write it all down_.

1) A colony of stick insects increases by 4% per week. Initially there are 30. How many will there be after 12 weeks?
2) The speed of a tennis ball rolled along a smooth floor falls by 16% every second. If the initial speed was 5 m/s find the speed after 20 seconds. How long will it take to stop?

Fractions and Decimals

On this page, you'll discover the delights of terminating and recurring decimals and experience the true joy of converting them into fractions.

Recurring or Terminating...

Recurring decimals have a pattern of numbers which repeats forever, e.g. ⅓ is the decimal 0.333333... Note, it doesn't have to be a single digit that repeats. You could have, for instance: 0.143143143.... Terminating decimals are finite, e.g. ½₀ is 0.05.

The denominator (bottom number) of a fraction tells you if it'll be a recurring or terminating decimal when you convert it. Fractions where the denominator has prime factors of only 2 or 5 will give terminating decimals. All other fractions will give recurring decimals.

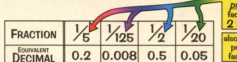

FRACTION	$\frac{1}{5}$	$\frac{1}{125}$	$\frac{1}{2}$	$\frac{1}{20}$
EQUIVALENT DECIMAL	0.2	0.008	0.5	0.05

only prime factors: **2 & 5**

also *other* prime factors

	$\frac{1}{7}$	$\frac{1}{35}$	$\frac{1}{3}$	$\frac{1}{6}$
	0.142857	0.0285714	0.3333	0.16666

For prime factors see p.34

Converting terminating decimals to fractions is very easy — you should be able to work out for yourself the very simple method from these examples:

$$0.6 = {}^{6}/_{10} \quad 0.3 = {}^{3}/_{10} \quad 0.7 = {}^{7}/_{10} \quad 0.45 = {}^{45}/_{100} \quad 0.05 = {}^{5}/_{100}, \text{ etc.}$$

$$0.345 = {}^{345}/_{1000} \quad 0.908 = {}^{908}/_{1000} \quad 0.024 = {}^{24}/_{1000} \quad 0.XYZ = {}^{XYZ}/_{1000}, \text{ etc.}$$

Recurring Decimals into Fractions

There's two ways to do it: 1) by UNDERSTANDING   2) by just LEARNING THE RESULT.

The Understanding Method:

1) Find the length of the repeating sequence and multiply by 10, 100, 1000, 10 000 or whatever to move it all up past the decimal point by one full repeated lump:
   E.g. $0.234234234... \times 1000 = 234.234234...$

2) Subtract the original number, r, from the new one (which in this case is 1000r)
   i.e. $1000r - r = 234.234234... - 0.234234... $ giving: $999r = 234$

3) Then just DIVIDE to leave r: $r = {}^{234}/_{999}$, and cancel if possible: $r = {}^{26}/_{111}$

The "Just Learning The Result" Method:

The fraction always has the repeating unit on the top and the same number of nines on the bottom — easy as that. Look at these and marvel at the elegant simplicity of it.

$$0.4444444 = 4/9 \qquad 0.34343434 = 34/99$$
$$0.124124124 = 124/999 \qquad 0.14561456 = 1456/9999$$

Always check if it will CANCEL DOWN of course, e.g. $0.363636... = 36/99 = 4/11.$

The Acid Test:
LEARN how to tell whether a fraction will be a terminating or recurring decimal, and all the methods above. Then turn over and write it all down.

1) Express 0.142857142857... as a fraction. 2) Without cheating, say if these fractions will give recurring or terminating decimals: a) 3/8 b) 9/280 c) 7/250

Manipulating Surds

RATIONAL NUMBERS The vast majority of numbers are rational. They are always either:

> 1) A whole number (either positive (+ve), or negative (–ve)), e.g. 4, -5, -12
> 2) A fraction p/q, where p and q are whole numbers (+ve or –ve), e.g. ¼, -½, ¾
> 3) A terminating or recurring decimal, e.g. 0.125, 0.3333333333..., 0.143143143143...

IRRATIONAL NUMBERS are messy!

> 1) They are always never-ending non-repeating decimals. π is irrational.
> 2) A good source of irrational numbers is square roots and cube roots.

Manipulating Surds

It sounds like something to do with controlling difficult children, but it isn't. Surds are expressions with irrational square roots in them. You **MUST USE THEM** if they ask you for an **EXACT** answer. There are a few simple rules to learn:

1) $\sqrt{a} \times \sqrt{b} = \sqrt{ab}$ e.g. $\sqrt{2} \times \sqrt{3} = \sqrt{2 \times 3} = \sqrt{6}$ — also $(\sqrt{b})^2 = b$, fairly obviously

2) $\dfrac{\sqrt{a}}{\sqrt{b}} = \sqrt{\dfrac{a}{b}}$ e.g. $\dfrac{\sqrt{8}}{\sqrt{2}} = \sqrt{\dfrac{8}{2}} = \sqrt{4} = 2$

3) $\sqrt{a} + \sqrt{b}$ — **NOTHING DOING**...   (in other words it is definitely **NOT** $\sqrt{a+b}$)

4) $(a + \sqrt{b})^2 = (a + \sqrt{b})(a + \sqrt{b}) = a^2 + 2a\sqrt{b} + b$ (**NOT** just $a^2 + (\sqrt{b})^2$)

5) $(a + \sqrt{b})(a - \sqrt{b}) = a^2 + a\sqrt{b} - a\sqrt{b} - (\sqrt{b})^2 = a^2 - b$

6) Express $\dfrac{3}{\sqrt{5}}$ in the form $\dfrac{a\sqrt{5}}{b}$ where a and b are whole numbers.
   To do this you must "**RATIONALISE the denominator**", which just means multiplying top and bottom by $\sqrt{5}$: $\dfrac{3\sqrt{5}}{\sqrt{5}\sqrt{5}} = \dfrac{3\sqrt{5}}{5}$ so a = 3 and b = 5

7) If you want an exact answer, **LEAVE THE SURDS IN**. As soon as you go using that calculator, you'll get a big fat rounding error — and you'll get the answer **WRONG**. Don't say I didn't warn you...

> **Example**: A square has an area of 15 cm². Find the length of one of its sides.
>
> **Answer**: The length of a side is $\sqrt{15}$ cm.
> If you have a calculator, then you can work out $\sqrt{15} = 3.8729833...$cm.
> If you're working without a calculator, or are asked to give an **EXACT** answer, then just write: $\sqrt{15}$ cm. That's all you have to do.

The Acid Test:
LEARN the 7 rules for manipulating surds, then turn over and write them all down.

Simplify 1) $(1 + \sqrt{2})^2 - (1 - \sqrt{2})^2$ 2) $(1 + \sqrt{2})^2 - (2\sqrt{2} - \sqrt{2})^2$

Algebraic Fractions

The Examiners like to throw nasty-looking algebraic fractions at you. But they're only trying to scare you because the rules for them are exactly the same as for ordinary fractions.

1) Cancelling

Cancel any bits that are multiplied on the top and bottom of a fraction (see p79 for more).

e.g. $\dfrac{x^2(x-3)}{x^5(x-3)^2} = \dfrac{x^2(x-3)}{x^5(x-3)^2} = \dfrac{x^2}{x^3(x-3)} = \dfrac{1}{x^3(x-3)}$

2) Multiplying

Multiply top and bottom separately and cancel if possible:

e.g. $\dfrac{st}{10w^3} \times \dfrac{35s^2tw}{6} = \dfrac{35s^3t^2w}{60w^3} = \dfrac{7s^3t^2}{12w^2}$

3) Dividing

Turn the second one upside down, then multiply and cancel if possible:

e.g. $\dfrac{12}{p+4} \div \dfrac{4(p-3)}{3(p+4)} = \dfrac{12^{\,3}}{p+4} \times \dfrac{3(p+4)}{4(p-3)} = \dfrac{9}{p-3}$

4) Adding/subtracting — not so easy

Always get a common denominator, i.e. same bottom line, and then ADD TOP LINES ONLY. For the common denominator, you're looking for the simplest expression that both bottom terms will divide into — this is usually just the two expressions multiplied together.

$\dfrac{t-2p}{3t-p} - \dfrac{1}{3} = \dfrac{3(t-2p)}{3(3t-p)} - \dfrac{1(3t-p)}{3(3t-p)} = \dfrac{3t-6p-3t+p}{3(3t-p)} = \dfrac{-5p}{3(3t-p)}$

EXAMPLE:

Write these as single fractions in their simplest form: a) $\dfrac{x}{wy} + \dfrac{y}{xw}$ b) $\dfrac{a^2}{b^{\frac{2}{3}}} + \dfrac{a^{-3}}{b^{\frac{1}{3}}}$

a) $\dfrac{x}{wy} + \dfrac{y}{xw} = \dfrac{xx}{wyx} + \dfrac{yy}{xwy} = \dfrac{x^2 + y^2}{xwy}$

The common denominator here is xwy because it's the simplest expression that wy and xw will both divide into.

b) $\dfrac{a^2}{b^{\frac{1}{3}}} \div \dfrac{a^{-3}}{b^{-\frac{2}{3}}} = \dfrac{a^2}{b^{\frac{1}{3}}} \times \dfrac{b^{-\frac{2}{3}}}{a^{-3}} = a^{(2--3)} \times b^{(-\frac{2}{3}-\frac{1}{3})} = \dfrac{a^5}{b}$

Turn the second fraction upside down and multiply it using rule 2 above. Then you need to carefully use the power laws (see p78) to simplify.

EXAMPLE: Solve $\dfrac{x}{x-6} + \dfrac{3}{x-3} = 1$

$\dfrac{x(x-6)(x-3)}{x-6} + \dfrac{3(x-6)(x-3)}{x-3} = (x-6)(x-3)$

Multiplying every term by $(x-6)$ and $(x-3)$ — this gets rid of the fractions right at the start.

$\Rightarrow x(x-3) + 3(x-6) = (x-6)(x-3)$

$\Rightarrow x^2 - 3x + 3x - 18 = x^2 - 9x + 18$

$\Rightarrow 9x = 36 \Rightarrow x = 4$

Note, you could have started by adding the fractions using rule 4 instead. It works out exactly the same.

The Acid Test:

Learn the Four Rules for dealing with Algebraic Fractions, then do the three examples below for yourself.

1) Simplify: a) $\dfrac{x^{\frac{1}{3}}}{y^{-1}} \times \dfrac{x^{-\frac{2}{3}}}{y^2}$ 2) Solve for x: $\dfrac{1}{2x} + \dfrac{x}{(x+1)} = 1$

Simultaneous Equations

For this module you need to be able to solve simultaneous equations where you have one linear and one quadratic equation. If the phrase "simultaneous equations" isn't ringing any bells in your skull, you'd better look at p60 from module 8 first...

Seven Steps For TRICKY Simultaneous Equations

Example: Solve these two simultaneous equations: $7x + y = 1$ and $2x^2 - y = 3$

1) Rearrange the quadratic equation so that you have the non-quadratic unknown on its own. Label the equations ① and ②.

$7x + y = 1$ — ①
$y = 2x^2 - 3$ — ②

2) Substitute the quadratic expression into the other equation. You'll get another equation — label it ③.

$7x + y = 1$ — ①
$y = 2x^2 - 3$ — ②
$7x + (2x^2 - 3) = 1$ — ③

In this example you just shove the expression for y into equation ①, in place of y.

3) Rearrange to get a quadratic equation. And guess what... You've got to solve it.

Remember — if it won't factorise, you can either use the formula or complete the square (see p.98-99).

$2x^2 + 7x - 4 = 0$

That factorises into $(2x - 1)(x + 4) = 0$

Check this step by multiplying out again:
$(2x - 1)(x + 4) = 2x^2 - x + 8x - 4 = 2x^2 + 7x - 4$ ☺

So, $2x - 1 = 0$ OR $x + 4 = 0$. In other words, x = 0.5 OR x = –4

4) Stick the first value back in one of the original equations (pick the easy one).

① $7x + y = 1$ Substitute in x = 0.5: $3.5 + y = 1$, so y = $1 - 3.5$ = –2.5

5) Stick the second value back in the same original equation (the easy one again).

① $7x + y = 1$ Substitute in x = –4: $-28 + y = 1$, so y = $1 + 28$ = 29

6) Substitute both pairs of answers back into the other original equation to check they work.

② $y = 2x^2 - 3$

Substitute in x = 0.5 and y = –2.5: $-2.5 = (2 \times 0.25) - 3 = -2.5$ — jolly good.
Substitute in x = –4 and y = 29: $29 = (2 \times 16) - 3 = 29$ — smashing.

7) Write the pairs of answers out again, *CLEARLY,* at the bottom of your working.

The two pairs of answers are: x = 0.5 and y = –2.5   or   x = –4 and y = 29

The Acid Test:
LEARN the 7 Steps for solving TRICKY Simultaneous Equations.

1) Apply the 7 steps to find x and y, given that:
a) $x = y^2 + 4$ and $x - 6y - 4 = 0$
b) $13y - x = -7$ and $3y^2 - x = 3$
c) $y^2 + x^2 = 9$ and $y + 2x = 0$
d) $x^2 + y^2 = 36$ and $4x = y + 6$

The Quadratic Formula

In module nine (p82), solving quadratic equations by factorising them was covered. Trouble is, factorising won't work unless you have nice whole number answers. But here's the big shock — there's actually a formula that will give you the solutions every single time:

The solutions to any quadratic equation $ax^2 + bx + c = 0$ are given by this formula:

$$x = \frac{-b \pm \sqrt{b^2 - 4ac}}{2a}$$

It's not the simplest of formulas. But you MUST LEARN IT if you want any chance of using it correctly in the exam. There are quite a few PITFALLS you must be wary of...

Using The Quadratic Formula

1) Always write it down in stages as you go. Take it nice and slowly — any fool can rush it and get it wrong, but there's no marks for being a clot.

2) MINUS SIGNS. Throughout the whole of algebra, minus signs cause untold misery because people keep forgetting them. In this formula, there are two minus signs that people keep forgetting: the -b and the -4ac.

The -4ac causes particular problems when either "a" or "c" is negative, because it makes the -4ac effectively +4ac — so learn to spot it as a HAZARD before it happens.

WHENEVER YOU GET A MINUS SIGN, THE ALARM BELLS SHOULD ALWAYS RING!

3) Remember you divide ALL of the top line by 2a, not just half of it.

4) Don't forget it's 2a on the bottom line, not just a. This is another common mistake.

EXAMPLE: "Find the solutions of $3x^2 + 7x = 1$ to 2 decimal places."

(The mention of decimal places in Exam questions is a very big clue to use the formula rather than trying to factorise it!)

METHOD:
1) First get it into the form $ax^2 + bx + c = 0$: $\quad 3x^2 + 7x - 1 = 0$
2) Then carefully identify a, b and c: $\quad a = 3, \quad b = 7, \quad c = -1$
3) Put these values into the quadratic formula and write down each stage:

$$x = \frac{-b \pm \sqrt{b^2 - 4ac}}{2a} \;=\; \frac{-7 \pm \sqrt{7^2 - 4 \times 3 \times -1}}{2 \times 3} \;=\; \frac{-7 \pm \sqrt{49 + 12}}{6}$$

$$= \frac{-7 \pm \sqrt{61}}{6} = \frac{-7 \pm 7.81}{6} = \textbf{0.1350 or -2.468}$$

So to 2 DP, the solutions are: $\quad \underline{x = 0.14 \text{ or } -2.47}$

4) Finally as a check put these values back into the original equation:
E.g. for x = 0.1350: $\quad 3 \times 0.135^2 + 7 \times 0.135 = 0.999675$,
which is 1, as near as ...

The Acid Test:

LEARN the 4 CRUCIAL DETAILS and the 4 STEPS OF THE METHOD for using the Quadratic Formula, then TURN OVER AND WRITE THEM ALL DOWN.

1) Find the solutions of these equations (to 2 DP) using the Quadratic formula:
a) $x^2 + 10x - 4 = 0$ b) $3x^2 - 3x = 2$ c) $(2x + 3)^2 = 15$

Completing the Square

$$x^2 + 12x - 5 = (x + 6)^2 - 41$$

The SQUARE...   ...COMPLETED

Solving Quadratics by "Completing The Square"

This is quite a clever way of solving quadratics, but it's perhaps a bit confusing at first. The name "Completing the Square" doesn't help — it's called that because you basically:

1) write down a SQUARED bracket, and then
2) stick a number on the end to "COMPLETE" it.

It's quite easy if you learn all the steps — some of them aren't all that obvious.

Method:

1) As always, REARRANGE THE QUADRATIC INTO THE STANDARD FORMAT:
$$ax^2 + bx + c = 0$$

2) If "a" is not 1 then divide the whole equation by "a" to make sure it is!

3) Now WRITE OUT THE INITIAL BRACKET: $(x + b/2)^2$

NB: THE NUMBER IN THE BRACKET is always HALF THE (NEW) VALUE OF "b"

4) MULTIPLY OUT THE BRACKETS and COMPARE TO THE ORIGINAL
to find what extra is needed, and add or subtract the adjusting amount.

Example: "Express $x^2 - 6x - 7 = 0$ as a completed square, and hence solve it."

The equation is already in the standard form and "a" = 1, so:

1) The coefficient of x is -6, so the squared brackets must be: $(x - 3)^2$

2) Square out the brackets: $x^2 - 6x + 9$, and compare to the original: $x^2 - 6x - 7$.
To make it like the original equation it needs -16 on the end, hence we get:

$(x - 3)^2 - 16 = 0$ as the alternative version of $x^2 - 6x - 7 = 0$

Don't forget though, we wish to SOLVE this equation, which entails these 3 special steps:

1) Take the 16 over to get: $(x - 3)^2 = 16$.

2) Then SQUARE ROOT BOTH SIDES: $(x - 3) = \pm 4$ AND DON'T FORGET THE $\pm$

3) Take the 3 over to get: $x = \pm 4 + 3$ so x = 7 or -1 (don't forget the $\pm$)

The Acid Test:
LEARN the 4 STEPS OF THE METHOD for completing the square and the 3 SPECIAL STEPS for SOLVING THE EQUATION you get from it.

1) Now turn over and write it all down to see what you've learned.   (Frightening isn't it.)
2) Find the solutions of these equations (to 2 d.p.) by completing the square:
   a) $x^2 + 8x - 9 = 0$ b) $x^2 + 14x = 11$ c) $x^2 + 10x - 4 = 0$

The Sine and Cosine Rules

Normal trigonometry using SOH CAH TOA etc. can only be applied to right-angled triangles. The Sine and Cosine Rules on the other hand allow you to tackle any triangle at all with ease.

Labelling The Triangle

This is very important. You must label the sides and angles properly so that the letters for the sides and angles correspond with each other:

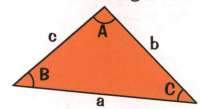

Remember, side "a" is opposite angle A etc.

It doesn't matter which sides you decide to call a, b, and c, just as long as the angles are then labelled properly.

Three Formulas to Learn:

These first two formulas let you work out sides and angles:

The Sine Rule

You don't use the whole thing with both "=" signs of course, so it's not half as bad as it looks — you just choose the two bits that you want:

$$\frac{a}{\text{SIN A}} = \frac{b}{\text{SIN B}} = \frac{c}{\text{SIN C}}$$

e.g. $\dfrac{b}{\text{SIN B}} = \dfrac{c}{\text{SIN C}}$ or $\dfrac{a}{\text{SIN A}} = \dfrac{b}{\text{SIN B}}$

The Cosine Rule

$$a^2 = b^2 + c^2 - 2bc\,\text{COS A}$$

or $\text{COS A} = \dfrac{b^2 + c^2 - a^2}{2bc}$

Area of the Triangle

Of course, you already know the simple formula when you have the base and vertical height:

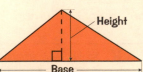

Area = ½ base × height

Well, here's a fancier formula that you can use when you know two sides and the angle between them:

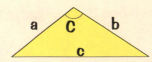

Area of triangle = ½ abSINC

You need to LEARN all of these formulas off by heart and practise using them. If you don't, you won't be able to use them in the Exam, even if they give them to you.

The Acid Test:

LEARN the proper labelling and the Three Formulas.

Now turn over and write down everything on this page.

The Sine and Cosine Rules

The Four Examples

Amazingly enough there are basically only <u>FOUR</u> question types where the SINE and COSINE rules would be applied. Learn the exact details of these four basic examples:

1) TWO ANGLES given plus ANY SIDE

— SINE RULE NEEDED

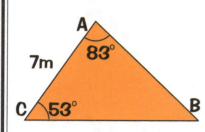

1) Don't forget the obvious: $B = 180 - 83 - 53 = \underline{44^0}$

2) Then use $\dfrac{b}{SIN B} = \dfrac{c}{SIN C}$ $\Rightarrow$ $\dfrac{7}{SIN 44} = \dfrac{c}{SIN 53}$

3) Which gives $\Rightarrow$ $c = \dfrac{7 \times SIN 53}{SIN 44} = \underline{8.05m}$

The rest is easy using the SINE RULE

2) TWO SIDES given plus an ANGLE NOT ENCLOSED by them

— SINE RULE NEEDED

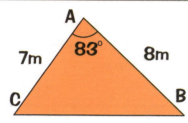

1) Use: $\dfrac{b}{SIN B} = \dfrac{c}{SIN C}$ $\Rightarrow$ $\dfrac{7}{SIN B} = \dfrac{8}{SIN 53}$

2) $\Rightarrow$ $SIN B = \dfrac{7 \times SIN 53}{8} = 0.6988$ $\Rightarrow B = SIN^{-1}(0.6988) = 44.3^0$

The rest is easy using the SINE RULE

3) TWO SIDES given plus THE ANGLE ENCLOSED by them

— COSINE RULE NEEDED

1) Use: $a^2 = b^2 + c^2 - 2bc\,COS A$

$= 7^2 + 8^2 - 2 \times 7 \times 8 \times COS 83$

$= 99.3506$ $\Rightarrow$ $a = \sqrt{99.3506} = \underline{9.97m}$

The rest is easy using the SINE RULE

4) ALL THREE SIDES given but NO ANGLES

— COSINE RULE NEEDED

1) Use: $COS A = \dfrac{b^2 + c^2 - a^2}{2bc}$

$= \dfrac{49 + 64 - 100}{2 \times 7 \times 8} = \dfrac{13}{112} = 0.11607$

2) Hence $A = COS^{-1}(0.11607) = \underline{83.3^0}$

The rest is easy using the SINE RULE

The Acid Test:
LEARN the FOUR BASIC TYPES as above.
Then cover the page and do these:

1) Write down <u>a new version</u> of each of the 4 examples above and then use the **SINE** and **COSINE RULES** to find <u>ALL of the sides and angles</u> for each one.

2) A triangle has two sides of 12m and 17m with an angle of 70^0 between them. Find all the other sides and angles in the triangle.   (A sketch is essential, of course).

The Graphs of Sin, Cos and Tan

You are expected to know these graphs and be able to sketch them <u>from memory</u>.
It really isn't that difficult — the secret is to notice their <u>similarities</u> and <u>differences</u>:

Y = SIN X

Y = COS X

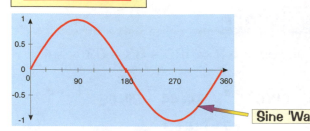

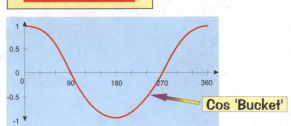

Sine 'Wave'

Cos 'Bucket'

1) <u>For 0° – 360°</u>, the shapes you get are a <u>SINE "WAVE"</u> (one peak, one trough) and a <u>COS "BUCKET"</u> (starts at the top, dips, and finishes at the top).

2) The underlying shape of both the SIN and COS graphs are <u>identical</u>, (as shown below) when you extend them (indefinitely) in both directions:

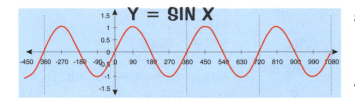

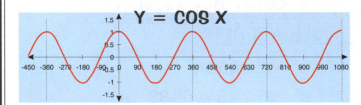

3) The only difference is that the SIN graph is shifted by 90° → compared to the COS graph.

4) Note that both graphs wiggle between <u>y-limits of exactly +1 and -1</u>.

5) The key to drawing the extended graphs is to first draw the 0 – 360° cycle of either the <u>SIN "WAVE"</u> or the <u>COS "BUCKET"</u> and then <u>repeat it</u> in <u>both directions</u> as shown.

Y = TAN X

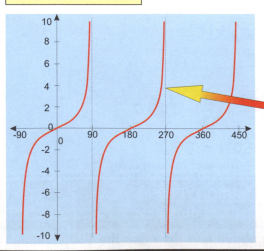

1) The TAN graph <u>BEARS NO RESEMBLANCE</u> to the other two.

2) It behaves in a fairly bizarre way at 90°, 270° etc. ....by disappearing up to <u>+ infinity</u> and then reappearing from <u>- infinity</u> on the other side of the <u>asymptote</u> (— a dotted line that the graph never quite touches).

3) So unlike the SIN and COS graphs, Y = TAN X is <u>not limited</u> to values between +1 and -1.

4) You'll also notice that whilst SIN and COS repeat <u>every 360°</u>, the TAN graph repeats <u>every 180°</u>.

The Acid Test:
LEARN the <u>FIVE graphs</u> above. <u>Then turn over and draw all five again in full detail.</u>

The Graphs of Sin, Cos and Tan

You can only do this if you've learnt the graphs on the other page:

SIN, COS and TAN for Angles of Any Size

There is ONE BASIC IDEA involved here:

> If you draw a horizontal line at a given value for sin x then it will pick out an infinite number of angles on the x-axis which all have the same value for sin x.

Example 1: "Find 6 different angles x such that sin x = 0.94"

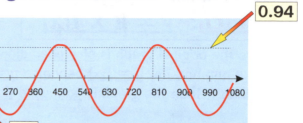

0.94

70°

Method

1) Sketch the extended sin x graph.

2) Put a horizontal line across at 0.94.

3) Draw lines down to the x-axis wherever the horizontal crosses the curve.

4) Use your calculator to find inv sin 0.94, to get the first angle (70° in this case).

5) The symmetry is surely obvious. You can see that 70° is 20° away from the peak, so all the other angles are clearly 20° either side of the peaks at 90°, 450°, etc.

> Hence we can say that sin x = +0.94 for all the following angles:
> ..... -290°, -250°, 70°, 110°, 430°, 470°, 790°, 830°....

Example 2: "Find three other angles which have the same cosine as 65°."

ANSWER: 1) Use the calculator to find COS 65° = +0.423.
2) Draw the extended COS curve and a horizontal line across at +0.423.
3) Draw the vertical lines from the intersections and use symmetry.

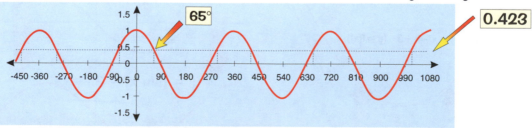

65°

0.423

Since 65° is 25° below 90° the other angles shown must be: -425°, -295°, -65°, etc.

The Acid Test:

LEARN the method above.
Then turn over and write it all down.

1) Find the first 4 positive values and first two negative values for x such that
   a) SIN x = 0.5   b) COS x = -0.67   c) TAN x = 1

Graph Transformations

Don't be put off by function notation involving f(x). It doesn't mean anything complicated, it's just a fancy way of saying "an equation in x".

In other words "y = f(x)" just means "y = some totally mundane equation in x, which we won't tell you, we'll just call it f(x) instead to see how many of you get in a flap about it".

In a question on transforming graphs they will either use function notation or they'll use a known function instead. There are only four different types of graph transformations so just learn them and be done with it. Here they are:

1) y-Stretch: $y = k \times f(x)$

This is where the original graph is stretched along the y-axis by multiplying the whole function by a number, i.e. y = f(x) becomes y = kf(x) (where k = 2 or 5 etc.). If k is less than 1, then the graph is squashed down in the y-direction instead:

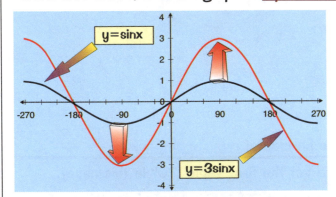

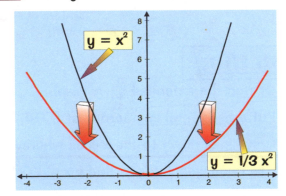

This graph shows y = f(x) and y = 3f(x)
(y = sin x and y = 3 sin x)

This graph shows y = f(x) and y = 1/3 f(x)
(y = x² and y = 1/3 x²)

2) y-Shift: $y = f(x) + a$

This is where the whole graph is slid up or down the y-axis with no distortion, and is achieved by simply adding a number onto the end of the equation: y = f(x) + a.

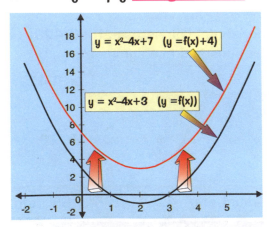

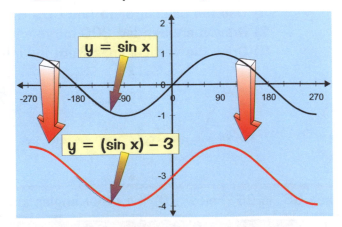

This shows y = f(x) and y = f(x) + 4
i.e. y = x² − 4x + 3, and
     y = (x² − 4x + 3) + 4
or y = x² − 4x + 7

This shows y = f(x) and y = f(x) − 3
i.e.   y = sin x and y = (sin x) − 3

Graph Transformations

3) x-Shift: y = f(x – a)

This is where the whole graph <u>slides to the left or right</u> and it only happens when you replace <u>"x"</u> everywhere in the equation <u>with "x – a"</u>. These are a bit tricky because they go "<u>the wrong way</u>". In other words if you want to go from <u>y = f(x)</u> to <u>y = f(x – a)</u> you must move the whole graph a distance "a" in the <u>positive</u> x-direction → (and vice versa).

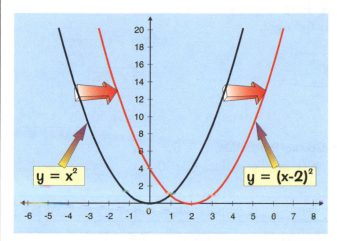

This graph shows <u>y = f(x)</u> and <u>y = f(x – 2)</u> (i.e. $y = x^2$ and $y = (x – 2)^2$)

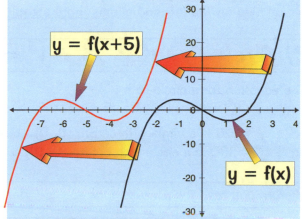

This graph shows <u>y = f(x)</u> and <u>y = f(x + 5)</u> i.e. $y = x^3 – 4x$, and $y = (x + 5)^3 – 4(x + 5)$

4) x-Stretch: y = f(kx)

These go "<u>the wrong way</u>" too — when k is a "<u>multiplier</u>" it <u>scrunches the graph up</u>, whereas when it's a "<u>divider</u>", it <u>stretches</u> the graph out. (The opposite of the y-stretch.)

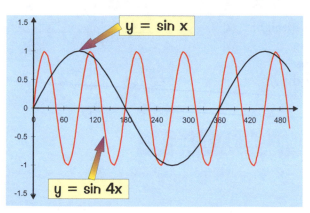

This graph shows
<u>y = sin x</u> and <u>y = sin(4x)</u>
The one that is all squashed up is
y = sin (4x). The way to sketch it
is simply that with a multiplier of 4,
it will be 4 times as squashed up.

(Each full cycle of up-and-down takes ¼ the amount of x-axis as the original graph, so you fit 4 of them into 1 of the other graph.)

Remember, if k is a <u>divider</u>, then the graph <u>spreads out</u>. So if the squashed up graph above was the original, <u>y = f(x)</u>, then the more spread out one would be <u>y = f(x/4)</u>.

The Acid Test:

LEARN the <u>Four types of Graph Transformations</u>, both the effect on the formula and the effect on the graph. <u>Then turn over</u> and <u>draw two examples of each type</u>.

Sketch these graphs: $y = x^2$ $y = x^2 – 4$ $y = 3x^2$ $y = (x – 3)^2$
$y = \cos x$ $y = \cos (x + 30^0)$ $y = \cos x + 3$ $y = 2\cos x – 4$

More Graphs

You need to know what <u>exponential</u> (kˣ) and <u>circle</u> graphs look like and how to plot them.

1) k^x Graphs: $y = k^x$, where k is some positive number

1) These graphs <u>curve upwards</u> when k > 1.

2) They're always <u>above the x-axis</u>.

3) They all <u>go through the point (0, 1)</u>.

4) For <u>bigger values of k</u>, the graph tails off towards zero <u>more quickly</u> on the left and <u>climbs more steeply</u> on the right.

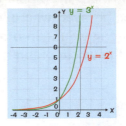

2) Circle Graphs: $x^2 + y^2 = r^2$

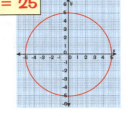

$x^2 + y^2 = 25$

The equation for a circle with <u>centre (0, 0)</u> and <u>radius r</u> is: $x^2 + y^2 = r^2$

$x^2 + y^2 = 25$ is a circle with centre (0, 0). $r^2 = 25$, so the radius, r, is 5.
$x^2 + y^2 = 100$ is a circle with centre (0, 0). $r^2 = 100$, so the radius, r, is 10.

Before you read the next bit, look at <u>page 61</u> on solving <u>simple</u> simultaneous equations <u>graphically</u>.

Simultaneous Equations and Graphs

EXAMPLE 1 — Two Graphs and Two Equations:

"By drawing graphs, solve the simultaneous equations $x^2 + y^2 = 16$ and $y = 2x + 1$."

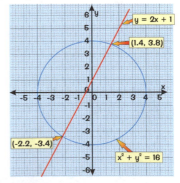

1) <u>DRAW BOTH GRAPHS</u> — $x^2 + y^2 = 16$ is the equation of a circle, centre (0, 0), radius 4 (see above).

2) <u>LOOK FOR WHERE THE GRAPHS CROSS</u> — The straight line crosses the circle at <u>two points</u>. Reading the <u>x and y values</u> of these points gives the solutions <u>x = 1.4, y = 3.8</u> and <u>x = -2.2, y = -3.4</u> (to 1 d.p.).

EXAMPLE 2 — Two Graphs but just One Equation, or so it seems...

"Using the graphs shown for $y = 4 + \frac{1}{2}x$ and $y = 6 - x^2/3$, solve the equation: $x^2/3 + \frac{1}{2}x - 2 = 0$."

<u>ANSWER</u>: <u>Learn</u> these important steps:

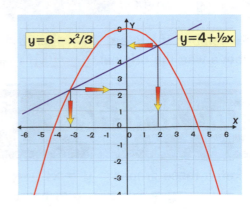

1) <u>Equating the equations</u> of the two graphs gives this:
$6 - x^2/3 = 4 + \frac{1}{2}x$ (a sort of "<u>merged</u> equation")

2) Now bring it all onto <u>one side</u> and you end up with:
$x^2/3 + \frac{1}{2}x - 2 = 0$ (the equation in the question!)

3) Hence the <u>solutions</u> to that equation are where the two initial equations ($y = 4 + \frac{1}{2}x$ and $y = 6 - x^2/3$) are <u>equal</u> — i.e. where their <u>graphs cross</u>, which as the graph shows is at: <u>x = 1.8</u> or <u>x = -3.3</u>. Splendid.

Volume and Surface Area

Stop! Don't take another step down this page until you've looked at p86 from module 9. You have to know all that module 9 stuff for this module too, so get it learned. When you've done that, this page will cover some extra bits on volume and area that will bring you pleasure beyond your wildest dreams.

A Frustum is Part of a Cone

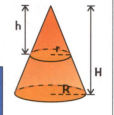

A <u>frustum of a cone</u> is what's left when the top part of a cone is cut off parallel to its circular base.

| VOLUME OF FRUSTUM | = | VOLUME OF THE ORIGINAL CONE | − | VOLUME OF THE REMOVED CONE | $= \frac{1}{3}\pi R^2 H - \frac{1}{3}\pi r^2 h$ |

Area of a Circle Segment

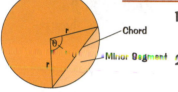

FINDING THE AREA OF A SEGMENT is OK if you know the formulas:

1) Find the <u>area of the sector</u> (using the formula from p86). $\boxed{\text{Area of Sector} = \frac{\theta}{360} \times \text{Area of full Circle}}$

2) Find the area of the triangle, then <u>subtract it</u> from the sector's area. (You can do this using the "½ abSINC" formula for the area of the triangle from page 100 which becomes: ½ r² SIN θ.)

Surface Area And Nets

1) <u>A NET</u> is just <u>A SOLID SHAPE FOLDED OUT FLAT</u>.

2) <u>SURFACE AREA OF A SOLID = AREA OF NET</u>.

3) <u>SPHERES, CYLINDERS AND CONES</u> have surface area formulas that you need to learn:

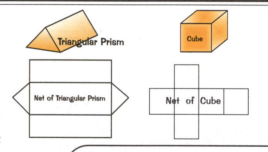

SPHERES:
Surface area = 4πr²

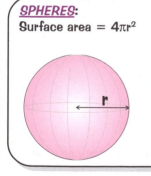

CONES:
Surface area = πrl + πr²

curved area of cone   area of circular base

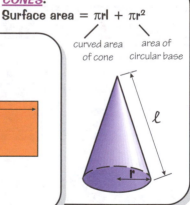

CYLINDERS:
Surface area = 2πrh + 2πr²

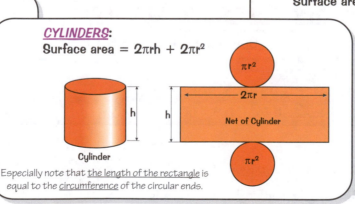

Net of Cylinder

Especially note that <u>the length of the rectangle</u> is equal to the <u>circumference</u> of the circular ends.

The Acid Test:

1) Calculate the surface area of a ball with a radius of 3 cm.
2) Find the surface area of a cylindrical can, height 12.5 cm, diameter 7.2 cm.
3) What solid can be constructed from this net? Calculate a) its surface area,
   b) its vertical height (if the blue circle is used as the base) c) its volume

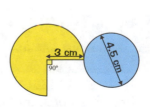

Congruence and Similarity

Congruence is another ridiculous maths word which sounds really complicated when it's not: If two shapes are congruent, they are simply the same — the same size and the same shape. That's all it is. They can however be mirror images.

CONGRUENT
— same size, same shape

SIMILAR
— same shape, different size

Note that the angles are always unchanged

Congruent Triangles — are they or aren't they?

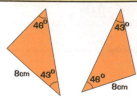

Probably the trickiest area of congruence is deciding whether two triangles, like the ones shown here, are CONGRUENT. In other words, from the skimpy information given, are the two going to be the same or different. There are THREE IMPORTANT STEPS:

1) The Golden Rule is definitely to draw them both in the same orientation — only then can you compare them properly:

2) Don't jump to hasty conclusions — although the 8cm sides are clearly in different positions, it's always possible that both top sides are 8cm.

In this case we can work out that they're not because the angles are different (so they can't be isosceles).

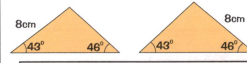

3) Now see if any of these conditions are true. If ONE of the conditions holds, the triangles are congruent.

1) SSS	three sides are the same
2) AAS	two angles and a side match up
3) SAS	two sides and the angle between them match up
4) RHS	a right angle, the hypotenuse (longest side) and one other side all match up

For two triangles to be congruent, ONE OR MORE of these four conditions must hold.

(If none are true, then you have proof that the triangles aren't congruent.)

Congruence and Transformations

Remember transformations? (See pages 18, 19 & 68 if you don't), well...

WHEN A SHAPE IS TRANSLATED, ROTATED OR REFLECTED, THE IMAGE IS CONGRUENT TO THE ORIGINAL SHAPE. ENLARGEMENTS DON'T FOLLOW THIS RULE.

e.g.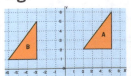

A to B is a translation of $\begin{pmatrix} -8 \\ -1 \end{pmatrix}$.
The lengths and angles are unchanged, so A is congruent to B.

e.g.

A to B is an enlargement of scale factor 2, and centre (2, 6).

The angles are unchanged but not the lengths, so A is not congruent to B.

The Acid Test:

LEARN the definitions of similarity and congruence, the 3 steps for checking for congruent triangles, and the rule about transformations.

Then, when you think you know it, turn the page over and write it all down again, from memory, including the sketches and examples.

Vectors

Three monstrously important things you need to know about <u>vectors</u>:

1) The Four Notations

The vector shown here can be referred to as:

$$\begin{pmatrix} 7 \\ 4 \end{pmatrix} \text{ or } \underset{\sim}{a} \text{ or } \mathbf{a} \text{ (in bold type) or } \overrightarrow{AB}$$

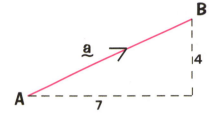

It's pretty obvious what these mean. Just make sure you know which is which in the column vector ($x\rightarrow$ and $y\uparrow$) and what a negative value means in a column vector.

2) Adding And Subtracting Vectors

Vectors must always be added <u>end to end</u>, so that the <u>arrows all point with</u> each other, <u>not against</u> each other.

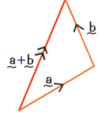
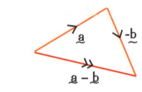
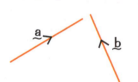

Adding and subtracting **COLUMN VECTORS** is really easy:

E.g. if $a = \begin{pmatrix} 5 \\ 3 \end{pmatrix}$ and $b = \begin{pmatrix} -2 \\ 4 \end{pmatrix}$ then $2a - b = 2\begin{pmatrix} 5 \\ 3 \end{pmatrix} - \begin{pmatrix} -2 \\ 4 \end{pmatrix} = \begin{pmatrix} 12 \\ 2 \end{pmatrix}$

3) A Typical Exam Question

This is a common type of question and it illustrates a very important vector technique:

To obtain the <u>unknown vector</u> just '<u>get there</u>' by any route <u>made up of known vectors</u>

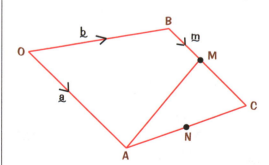

Applying this rule we can easily obtain the following vectors in term of $\underset{\sim}{a}$, $\underset{\sim}{b}$ and $\underset{\sim}{m}$ (given that M and N are mid points):

1) $\overrightarrow{AM} = -\underset{\sim}{a} + \underset{\sim}{b} + \underset{\sim}{m}$ (i.e. get there via O and B)

2) $\overrightarrow{OC} = \underset{\sim}{b} + 2\underset{\sim}{m}$ (i.e. get there via B and M)

3) $\overrightarrow{AC} = -\underset{\sim}{a} + \underset{\sim}{b} + 2\underset{\sim}{m}$ (A to C via O, B and M)

The Acid Test:

LEARN the important details on this page, then <u>turn over and write them down.</u>

1) For the diagram above, express the following in terms of $\underset{\sim}{a}, \underset{\sim}{b}$ and $\underset{\sim}{m}$:

a) $\overrightarrow{MO}$ b) $\overrightarrow{AN}$ c) $\overrightarrow{BN}$ d) $\overrightarrow{NM}$

Time Series

Time Series — Measure the Same Thing over a Period of Time

A time series is what you get if you measure the
same thing at a number of different times.

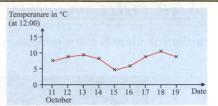

EXAMPLE: Measuring the temperature in your greenhouse at
12 o'clock each day gives you a time series — other
examples might be profit figures, crime figures or rainfall.

THE RETAIL PRICE INDEX (RPI) IS A TIME SERIES: Every month, the prices of loads of items (same ones
each month) — are combined to get an index number called the RPI, which is a kind of average.
As goods get more expensive, this index number gets higher and higher. So when you see on TV that inflation this
month is 2.5%, what it actually means is that the RPI is increasing at an annual rate of 2.5%.

Seasonality — The Same Basic Pattern

This is when there's a definite pattern that **REPEATS ITSELF** every so often.
This is called **SEASONALITY** and the "so often" is called the **PERIOD**.

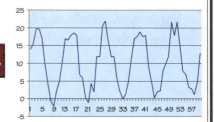

To find the PERIOD, measure PEAK TO PEAK (or trough to trough).

This series has a period of 12 months. There are a few irregularities,
so the pattern isn't exactly the same every 12 months, but it's about right.

Trend — Ignoring the Wrinkles

This time series has lots of random fluctuations
but there's a definite upwards trend.
The pink line is the trend line.
It's straight, so this is a linear trend.

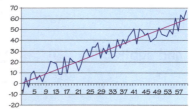

Moving Average — Smooths Out the Seasonality

It's easier to spot a trend if you can 'get rid of' the seasonality and some of the irregularities.

One way to smooth the series is to use a moving average.

This is a time series that definitely looks
periodic — but it's
difficult to tell if
there's a trend.

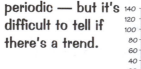

... but plot the
moving average
(in pink — must be pink —
that's dead important)...

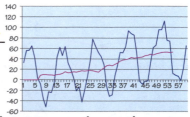

The period is 12, so you
use 12 values for the
moving average:

...and you can easily see the upward
trend.

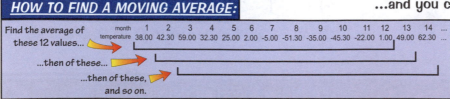

HOW TO FIND A MOVING AVERAGE:

Find the average of
these 12 values...
...then of these...
...then of these,
and so on.

month	1	2	3	4	5	6	7	8	9	10	11	12	13	14	...
temperature	38.00	42.30	59.00	32.30	25.00	2.00	-5.00	-51.30	-35.00	-45.30	-22.00	1.00	49.00	62.30	...

The Acid Test:
LEARN the words TIME SERIES, SEASONALITY, PERIOD, TREND,
MOVING AVERAGE. Cover the page and write a description of each.

1) My town's rainfall is measured every month for 20 yrs and graphed. There's a rough pattern, which repeats
itself every 4 months. a) What is the period of this time series? b) Describe how to calculate a moving average.

Revision Summary for Module Ten

Wahoo! The last page of work in the book. And it's quite a meaty page to finish on. But before you start these questions you need to read the following pages from previous modules. You need these for Module 10 too:

- Spread of data (page 75 module 8)   - Probability (page 89 module 9)

1) What is the formula for compound growth and decay?

2) Demonstrate the simple method for converting terminating decimals to fractions.

3) Demonstrate a not-so-simple method for converting recurring decimals to fractions.

4) Name three different forms that a rational number can take, and give examples.

5) Explain how irrational numbers are different from rational numbers.

6) Write down seven key points to do with manipulating surds.

7) Use examples to show how to cancel, multiply, divide, add and subtract with algebraic fractions.

8) What are the seven steps for doing simultaneous equations where one's quadratic?

9) Write down the formula for solving quadratic equations. What clue tells you that you need it?

10) What are the three main pitfalls that catch people out with the quadratic formula?

11) What are the four main steps for turning a quadratic into a "completed square"?

12) Write down the formulas for the sine and cosine rules and draw a labelled triangle to show what the letters in the formulas represent.

13) What's the formula for the area of a triangle if you know 2 sides and the angle between them?

14) There are four different situations where the sine and cosine rules may be used.
Do a sketch of each one, say which rule should be used and write down the formula.

15) Sketch the graphs of sin x, cos x and tan x for the range –180° to 540°.

16) What does the notation $y = f(x)$ mean? Is it really complicated?

17) Name the four types of transformation you can apply to graphs.

18) Sketch examples of each of the four transformations by modifying $y = x^2$. Label each graph.

19) Write down the general equations of exponential and circle graphs. Sketch examples for each.

20) Explain how to solve a pair of simultaneous equations using graphs.

21) What is a frustum, and how do you calculate its volume?

22) Write down the surface area formulas for a sphere, a cylinder and a cone?

23) What do congruent and similar mean?

24) What four conditions can be used to see whether two triangles are congruent?

25) For each of the four transformations, say if the transformed shape is congruent to the original.

26) What are the four vector notations? What's the main rule for adding or subtracting vectors?

27) In a typical exam question, what's the basic rule for finding an unknown vector?

28) Which one of the following is not a time series?

   a) Measuring the temperature in 20 different countries at 12:00 today, GMT.

   b) Measuring the temperature in Britain at 12:00 every day for 100 days.

   c) The Retail Price Index.

29) How do you calculate the period of a seasonal time series?

30) Describe the method for finding out whether a seasonal time series has an overall trend.

Answers

Module Six

P.1 Rounding and Estimating: **1) a)** 3.2 **b)** 1.8 **c)** 2.3 **d)** 0.5 **2) a)** 350 **b)** 500 **c)** 12.4 **d)** 0.036

P.3-4 Multiplying and Dividing Without a Calculator: **1) a)** 336 **b)** 616 **c)** 832 **d)** 6.325 **e)** 34.56
2) a) 45 **b)** 64 **c)** 59   **P.4**: **1)** 1.2   **2)** 12.1   **3)** 1.2   **4)** 56   **5)** 46   **6)** 12

P.5 Fractions: **1) a)** 5/32 **b)** 32/35 **c)** 1 3/20 **2) a)** 3/8 **b)** £1.75   **3)** 2/5, 3/8, 1/4

P.7 Calculator Buttons: **1) a)** 11/4 **b)** 33/2 **c)** 33/4   **2) a)** 1.70 **b)** 39.96

P.8 Ratio: **1)** 56p   **2)** £1000 : £1400

P.9 Ratio: **1)** Weight per penny: 150g tin is 1.7 g/p, 250 g tin is 1.8 g/p, 750g tin is 1.9 g/p, so 750g tin is the best value.

P.10 Algebra: **1) a)** $2x - 4$ **b)** $5x + x^2$ **c)** $y^2 + xy$ **d)** $-6 - 2z$ **2) a)** $5(xy + 1)$ **b)** $a(5 - 7b)$
c) $x(4 + x)$ **d)** $y^2(y + 2)$

P.12 Drawing Graphs from Equations: **2)**

x	-4	-2	-1	0	1	2	4
y	-6	-4	-3	-2	-1	0	2

3)

P.13 Polygons: **1)** Exterior angles = 60°, interior angles = 120° **2)** 360° **3)** 540°

P.14 Parallel Lines: **1)** 120° and 60° all round

P.15 Areas: **1) a)** 10cm² **b)** 5cm²
c) First, find D = 1.91cm. D is twice r, so r = 0.95cm.
Which means Area = 2.86cm² (2.d.p.)

P.16 Perimeter, Area and Volume: **1)** 69 cm²

P.17 Surface Area, Nets and Projections: **1)** 340 cm²

P.19 The Four Transformations: **1)** A → B Rotation ¼ turn clockwise about the origin.   **2)** B → C reflection in the line Y=X.   **3)** C → A reflection in the y-axis.   **4)** A → D translation of 9 left and 7 down

P.20 Drawing Triangles: **1)** Check all angles equal 60°.   **2)** Check the angle between the 3cm and 4cm line is a right angle.   **3)** BC = 6cm

P.22 Probability: **1) a)** 1/13 **b)** 6/13 **c)** 3/26

P.24 Scatter Graphs: **1)** The two things are not closely related. There is no correlation.

P.25 Frequency Tables: See right.
Mean = 2.5, Mode = 2, Range = 6

No. of Phones	0	1	2	3	4	5	6	TOTALS
Frequency	1	25	53	34	22	5	1	141
No. × Frequency	0	25	106	102	88	25	6	352

Module Seven

P.27 Powers: **1) a)** 3^8 **b)** 4 **c)** 8^{12} **d)** 1 **e)** 7^6 **2) a)** 5^{12} **b)** 36 or 6^2 **c)** 2^5

P.28 Square Roots and Cube Roots: **1) a)** 14.14 **b)** 20, other val in a) is -14.14
2) a) g = 6 or -6 **b)** b = 4 **c)** r = 3 or -3

P.29 Estimating and Checking: 1) 2

P.31 Ratio: **1) a)** 5:7 **b)** 2:3 **c)** 3:5   **2)** 17½ bowls of porridge   **3)** £3500 : £2100 : £2800

P.32 Percentage Problems: **1)** Vat = 22 / 100 × 65 = 14.3, so total cost = 65 + 14.3 = £79.30
2) Price after discount = 20 /100 × 0.75 = £0.15

P.33 Prime Numbers: **1) a)** 101, 103, 107, 109   **b)** none   **c)** 503, 509

P.34 HCF, LCM and Prime Factors: **1)** 18   **2)** 12   **3) a)** $2 \times 5 \times 3 \times 3 \times 11$ **b)** $2 \times 2 \times 2 \times 2 \times 2 \times 5$

P.35 Number Sequences: **1) a)** 20, 27 "Add one extra each time" **b)** 2,000 20,000 "Multiply the previous term by 10" **c)** 4, 2 "Divide the previous term by 2"   **2)** 2n + 5

P.36 Making Formulas from Words: **1)** $y = 5x - 3$, $y = -13$ **2)** C = 95n

P.37 Solving Equations: **1) a)** $x = -½$ **b)** $x = 5$ **2)** $b = ½a + 3$

P.38 Algebra: **1)** $x^2 + 8x + 7$ **2)** $x^2 + 2x - 3$ **3)** $x^2 + 4x - 12$ **4)** $x^2 - 9x + 20$

P.39 Quadratic Graphs: See graph. Using graph, solutions are x = -2 and x = 3.

P.40 Inequalities: **1)** $x \geq -2$ **2)** $x \geq -4$, $x < 2$, x = -4, -3, -2, -1, 0, 1

Answers

P.41 Trial and Improvement: **1)** x = 1.6

P.42 Angle Problems: **1)** $w = 30°$, $x = 90°$, $y = 109°$, $z = 71°$

P.43 Pythagoras' Theorem:

1) BC = 8m   **2)** 7m, 24m, 25m is a right angled triangle because $a^2 + b^2 = h^2$ works.

P.44 Volume and Converting Measures: **1) a)** Trapezoidal Prism, $V = 148.5$ cm^3 **b)** Cylinder, $V = 0.700$ m^3 or 700 000 cm^3 **2) a)** 230,000 cm^2 **b)** 3.45 m^2 **c)** 5,200,000 cm^3 **d)** 0.1 m^3

P.45 Coordinates: **1)** (3, 5)   **2)** (5, 1)   **3)** A = (7, 0, 0), C = (0, 4, 0), E = (7, 0, 2)

P.47 Loci and Constructions: **1)** See right.

P.49 Speed and Density:

1) Density = Mass ÷ Volume   **2)** 16.5 g/cm^3 **3)** 603g   **4)** Speed = Distance ÷ Time   **5)** Time = 7½ hrs Dist = 11.2km

P.50 Probability — Relative Frequency:

1) Landing on red: 0.43, landing on blue: 0.24, landing on green: 0.33

P.51-52 Grouped Frequency Tables:

1) a) Discrete, possible table: Columns "Shoe Size" and "frequency", Shoe size intervals: 3, 4, 5, 6, 7, 8, 9, 10 , 11, 12. **b)** Continuous, possible table: Columns "Height (cm)" and "frequency", intervals: $140 \le h < 150$, $150 \le h < 160$, $160 \le h < 170$, etc.

P.52 (See table to the right.)
1) Mean = 17.4 cm **2)** Modal Group = $17.5 \le L < 18.5$

Length L (cm)	15.5≤L<16.5	16.5≤L<17.5	17.5≤L<18.5	18.5≤L<19.5	TOTALS
Frequency	12	18	23	8	61
Mid-Interval Value	16	17	18	19	
Freq × MIV	192	308	414	152	1064

Module Eight

P.55 Standard Index Form: **2)** 9.58×10^5 **3)** 1.8×10^{-4} **4)** 4560   **5)** 2×10^{21} , 2,000,00.....(21 zeros!)

P.56 Percentage Problems: **1)** 40% **2)** £20,500 **3)** £19.68

P.57 Basic Algebra: **1) a)** $5x^2 - 15x$ **b)** $6x^2 + 10x - 4$ **c)** $2x^2 + 24x + 36$

P.58 Solving Equations: **1)a)** x = 2   **b)** x = - 0.2 or -1/5   **c)** x = ±3

P.59 Rearranging Formulas: **1)** C = 5(F − 32)/9   **2) a)** p = -4y/3   **b)** p = rq/(r + q)   **c)** p = ±√{rq/(r + q)}

P.60 Simultaneous Equations: **2)** F = 3, G = -1

P.61 Simultaneous Equations with Graphs: **2) a)** x=2, y=4   **b)** x=1½, y=3

P.62 Quadratic Equations: **1a)** x = 3 or -8 **b)** x = 7 or -1

P.63 Graphical Inequalities: **1)** See right.

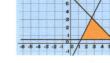

P.65 Straight Lines: **1)**

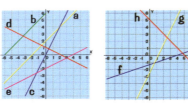 

P.66: **1)** -1.5

P.68 Combinations of Transformations: **1)** C→D, Reflection in the y-axis, and an enlargement SF 2, centre the origin,   D→C, Reflection in the y-axis, and an enlargement SF ½, centre the origin.   **2)** A'→B,   Rotation of 180° clockwise or anticlockwise about the point (0,3).

p.69 Enlargements and Dimensional Analysis: **1)** A'(-3,-1.5),   B'(-7.5,-3), C'(-6,-6) **2)** πr^2 = Area, Lwh = Volume, πd = Perimeter, ½bh = Area, 2bh + 4lh = Area, $4r^2h + 3\pi d^3$ = Volume, $2\pi r(3L + 5T)$ = Area

P.71 Trigonometry — Sin, Cos, Tan: **1)** x = 26.5 m   **2)** 23.6°   **3)** 32.6° (both)

P.72-73 Probability — Tree Diagrams: **1)** $\frac{12}{25}$ **P.73:** **1)** 0.51

Answers

P.74 Cumulative Frequency: **1)**

No. of fish	41 – 45	46 – 50	51 – 55	56 – 60	61 – 65	66 – 70	71 – 75
Frequency	2	7	17	25	19	8	2
Cum. Freq.	2	9	26	51	70	78	80

2) and 3)

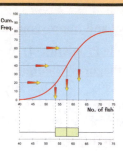

Median = 58, Lower Quartile = 53, Upper Quartile = 62, Interquartile range = 9

Module Nine

P.77 Calculation Bounds: **1) a)** x could be from 2.315 to 2.325, y is 0.445 to 0.455   **b)** max z = 4.57 (3 s.f.), min z = 4.51 (3 s.f.)

P.78 Powers: **1) a)** 4^8 **b)** 3^3 **c)** 2^{12} **d)** 2^6 **e)** 6^6
2) a) 64   **b)** 1/625   **c)** 1/5   **d)** 2   **e)** 125   **f)** 1/25   **3) a)** 1.53×10^{17} **b)** 15.9   **c)** 2.89

P.79 Basic Algebra: **1)** $4xyz(3x + y)$ **2)** $(x - 3) / (x - 5)$

P.80 Direct and Inverse Proportion: **1) a)** E.g. Total cost vs No. of tins of Bone-tingling Fireball Soup   **b)** E.g. no. of people working on a job vs time taken to complete it.

P.81 Direct and Inverse Proportion: **1) a)** 0.632 Hz   **b)** 40.8 cm

P.82 Quadratic Equations: **1) a)** x = 4 or -3/5   **b)** x = 1/3 or -3/2   **c)** x = 1 or 5/8

P.83 Straight Lines: **1)** y = 2x + 2   **2)** y = -½x + 4

P.85 Circle Geometry: **1)** BCD = 90°, CBO = 42°, OBE = 48°, BOE = 84°, OEF = 90°, AEB = 42°, DOE = 96°

P.86 Volume: **1)** Cone, 20.3 m³   **2)** Perimeter 27.5 cm, area 35 cm²

P.87 Enlargements and Line Segments: **1)** 42.4cm tall (to 3.s.f.)   **2)** 64m²   **3)** 5.66 units

P.88 3D Pythagoras and Trigonometry: **1)** 25.1°   **2)** 7.07 cm

P.89 Probability: **1) a)** Probability = QQA+QAQ+AQQ = (4/52)(3/51)(1/50) + (4/52)(1/51)(3/50) + (1/52)(4/51)(3/50) = 3/11050   **b)** Probability = (4/52) × (3/51) + (4/52) × (3/51) + (4/52) × (3/51) = 3 × (4/52) × (3/51) = 3/221

P.90 Histograms: **1)** 0–5: 9,   5–10: 27,   10–15: 36,   15–20: 45,   20–25: 27,   25–35: 18,   35–55: 18,   55–65: 36,   65–80: 162,   80–90: 126,   90–100: 18

P.91 Sampling Methods: **1)** Sample too small, motorways not representative of average motorist, only done at one time of day and in one place. Better approach: Take samples from a range of different locations across the country, take samples at different times of day, have a much larger sample size, e.g. 1000.

Module Ten

P.93 Compound Growth and Decay: **1)** 48 stick insects   **2)** 0.15 m/s. Forever.

P.94 Fractions: **1)** 1/7   **2) a)** terminating **b)** recurring **c)** terminating

P.95 Manipulating Surds: **1)** $4\sqrt{2}$ **2)** $1 + 2\sqrt{2}$

P.96 Algebraic Fractions: **1)** $\dfrac{x^{-1}}{y}$ **2)** x = 1

P.97 Simultaneous Equations: **1) a)** x = 4, y = 0 or x = 40, y = 6   **b)** x = -5/3, y = -2/3 or x = 72, y = 5
c) $x = 3/\sqrt{5}, y = -6/\sqrt{5}$ or $x = -3/\sqrt{5}, y = 6/\sqrt{5}$ **d)** x = 0, y = -6 or x = 48/17, y = 90/17

P.98 The Quadratic Formula: **1) a)** x = 0.39 or -10.39   **b)** x = 1.46 or -0.46   **c)** x = 0.44 or -3.44

P.99 Completing the Square: **2) a)** x = 1 or -9   **b)** x = 0.75 or -14.75 (2 d.p.)   **c)** x = 0.39 or -10.39 (2 d.p.)

P.101 The Sine and Cosine Rules: **2)** 17.13m, 68.8°, 41.2°

P.103 The Graphs of Sin, Cos and Tan: **1) a)** x = -330°, -210°, 30°, 150°, 390°, 510°   **b)** x = -228°, -132°, 132°, 228°, 492°, 588°   **c)** x = -315°, -135°, 45°, 225°, 405°, 585°

P.105 Graph Transformations: See right.

P.107 Volume and Surface Area:
1) 113.1 cm² (1.d.p.)   **2)** 364 cm²   **3)** A cone
a) 37.1 cm² (3.s.f.)   **b)** 1.98 cm (3.s.f.)   **c)** 10.5 cm³ (3 s.f.)

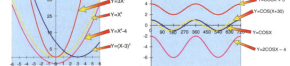

P.109 Vectors: **1) a)** $-\mathbf{m} - \mathbf{b}$ **b)** $\frac{1}{2}\mathbf{b} - \frac{1}{2}\mathbf{a} + \mathbf{m}$ (=½AC)   **c)** $\frac{1}{2}(\mathbf{a} - \mathbf{b}) + \mathbf{m}$ **d)** $\frac{1}{2}(\mathbf{b} - \mathbf{a})$

P.110 Time Series: **1) a)** period = 4 months   **b)** Find the average of the readings from months 1-4, then the average from months 2-5, then from months 3-6, etc. (and you could plot these on a graph to see the trend).

Index

Index

MRHR41